BR

THE GLASS SLIPPER

BREAKING
THE GLASS SLIPPER

Debunking the Myths that Hold Women Back

By

ELAINE TURNER

FREE EFFORTLESSLY GLAMOROUS INSIDER RESOURCES

Thank you for purchasing *Breaking the Glass Slipper*.
To receive special updates from Elaine, lifestyle insights, and exclusive coupons for ElaineTurner.com, sign up at:
ElaineTurner.com/book

Access your insider resources now so you don't forget!

The information provided in this book is designed to provide helpful information about the subjects discussed. The author and publisher disclaim any and all liability associated with the recommendations and guidelines set forth in this book. There are no guarantees implied or expressed from the information or principles contained in this book. Individual results will vary.

Printed in the United States of America
ISBN:978-0-692-14964-5
Published By: E&J COMMUNICATIONS

To my daughter Marlie, you are the light that shines through my cracks. The light that inspires me to find grace. To keep searching for peace. To know and practice compassion daily. And most of all, to LOVE wholeheartedly in all things perfectly imperfect.

ABOUT THE AUTHOR

Elaine Turner is many things—a designer, entrepreneur, mother, wife, sister, daughter, philanthropist and best girlfriend. You can also find her moonlighting as a part-time author, comedian, psychologist and interior designer. But all these so-called roles only tell part of the story, Elaine's heart beats through connection with other people. So first and foremost, Elaine's a lover of people.

In April of 2000, she co-founded her company and brand, Elaine Turner Designs, with her husband Jim Turner. What started out as mainly an entrepreneurial, creative pursuit has since morphed into a much a deeper mission. A mission of hope. A mission inspired by her mother's 30-year-long battle with breast cancer and her daughter's genetic condition that allows Elaine to use her fashion platform as a vehicle toward changing lives and making a difference. A mission of inspiring women to use their voices for good. To come together, expose their cracks, share their wounds and lift each other up in the process. Elaine lives in Houston, Texas with her husband and their two children, Harrison and Marlie.

CONTENTS

PREFACE

"Ideas arrive when people are ready. Ideas hold their own energy that can pass from one person to another."

—*Elizabeth Gilbert,* Big Magic

Have you ever experienced "in-the-moment fate"? I'm not talking about spotting a Whataburger sign in the distance on a cold, dark night just as you fall victim to extreme hunger. I'm talking about fate that you could feel as it unfolded. I like to call it "goosebump fate." It is a moment in life that is so profound that it heightens all senses in your body and leaves physical traces you can't ignore. Goosebumps.

I've experienced it.

In fact, goosebump fate is what got me here. Writing this book.

In spring 2017 I was in Dallas visiting the Elaine Turner store in Plano. It was going to be a crazy couple of days filled with obligations and commitments, and we had an early morning TV appearance on *Good Morning Texas* to showcase our new Spring collection. The collection was inspired by Havana, Cuba, and was full of vibrant colors, tropical details and bold prints. I was a little stressed about the whole thing and unsure of how it would go; television can be very unpredictable. Luckily, the segment came off well, and we actually saw incredible results from the experience. I remember feeling a moment of relief after it was all done, and I was ready to visit our Plano store for a highly anticipated event we were hosting that afternoon. As I walked into the store, I saw beautiful women and smiles as far as I could see. Our event that day was raising money and awareness for the Dallas/Fort Worth Alopecia Foundation. Alopecia is an autoimmune disease that causes extreme hair loss. It's a very rare, complicated and enigmatic disease.

The event was hosted by a mother whose 12-year-old daughter had the disease. Her child was in middle school and completely bald. I felt truly connected to the woman as she told me about her daughter. We shared our similar experiences about how our daughters both deal with differences. As far as I could tell, the event was unfolding to be even more than I could have expected; we were meeting lovely people, selling a lot of product and supporting an incredible cause. Little did I know, there was more to come . . . .

As I was talking with one of the hosts, I noticed a woman walk out of the dressing room. She was an older, beautiful woman with short gray hair. I didn't think much of it, but I did notice she wasn't necessarily a part of the group that was there. It was almost time for me to leave and head to the airport, but as I was walking toward the back to grab my purse, I heard a soft, sweet voice say, "Elaine." I turned around and it was her.

As I walked closer to her, I saw her face was especially sweet, gentle and soft. She smiled and hugged me. I looked at her and noticed her eyes glistening. I saw her hair was thinning and assumed she also had alopecia. She began talking to me and everything around me fell silent. I was utterly and completely present to her. It was as if something divine was taking place; time stopped and I knew I needed to be there for her. She started off by telling me that she saw our segment on TV earlier that morning and how it had made a huge impact on her. She told me she had woken up that morning feeling "awful," as she put it, and felt weak and in pain. She said she was pouring herself a cup of coffee when she turned around and saw me on TV talking about our Havana-inspired looks of the season. She then told me she sat down and felt an immediate positive energy come over her. She said, "Elaine, the colors and beautiful clothes and accessories captivated me." She told me how much she loved the silhouettes and how they appeared to fit most body types.

As she continued talking, I kept thinking to myself, *There has to be something more happening here. This can't just be about fashion.* I thanked her many times for her compliments on the collection, but then she nervously grabbed my hand and abruptly said, "Elaine, there's something more. I hope it's OK if I share this with you." My heart was pounding and I said, "Yes, it's OK, you can tell me."

She then very softly said, “I’m dying of multiple myeloma.” Well, as you can imagine, I was speechless. I froze and tears started to well up in my eyes. She went on to tell me she had just received the news earlier in the week that her scans had come back showing new cancer growth and multiple lesions were detected in different parts of her body. The doctors weren’t sure there was any more they could do for her and told her to start preparing for her death.

I was stunned. I couldn’t believe what I was hearing. I kept thinking, *Wait, I’m a fashion designer! Is this woman really telling me this?* It felt surreal. I wasn’t sure what to do, but my instinct was to immediately hug her, and she hugged me back. We were both silent for a minute, and I looked up at her and saw tears streaming down her face. As she pulled away, she said something to me that I’ve never been told in almost 20 years of owning my business: “Elaine, don’t ever underestimate what you do. Your clothes and accessories brought me hope this morning. The bright colors and feminine styles spoke to me.” And then she finished with “I knew this is what I wanted to wear as I finished out my time here on Earth.” Well, to say the least, I started to cry. It’s ironic, actually, because I felt happiness and complete grief at the same time. I guess the happiness stemmed from the idea that I could provide her with some joy, even if only for a temporary time, and I felt grief from the pure tragedy of it all.

Needless to say, I stayed a little longer and helped her put together several outfits, and in that moment, I could see pure joy emanate from her as she tried things on and laughed and danced around the fitting room. She was so happy! I've never felt more fulfilled in all my years of being a business owner. I knew I was witnessing a "God" moment. A moment for us to share: our shared wounds, our shared joy and our shared humanity. It was a gift to be fully present with her as she relished the moment of feeling alive, beautiful and happy.

A year later, *Breaking the Glass Slipper* was born. I knew that day last April held a message within it—a message of hope. The realization that the clothes and accessories I create could bring a terminally ill woman out of the darkness and into the light to such a degree sparked an idea deep inside of me, an idea to explore in more depth the complex journey we go on as women. Truthfully, the misguided assumptions we make about the role fashion can play in our lives was only the beginning. I also felt compelled to look deeper into the falsehoods we are programmed to believe surrounding the roles we take on as women, and how we perceive ourselves and other women around us.

We are going to tackle some universal themes in this book about the challenges we face being women in the 21st century. Our innate desire to please and seek perfection, coupled with the ambiguous expectations that confront us as women, creates an overwhelming sense of lack. My hope is to embark on a journey with you in the next *180 pages or so* that allows us to see through a fresh lens of hope, clarity and togetherness.

In each chapter, I explore, deconstruct, analyze and ultimately debunk a pervasive myth. I conclude the chapters with prompting questions to encourage a time for self-reflection and discovery. I have come to understand and embrace that the questions we ask ourselves are often more important than the quest for clear answers. Asking the right questions is a chance for deeper understanding and self-realization, and as a result, we can hopefully find some peace, healing and self-fulfillment. I am thankful you are on this ride with me asking the hard questions, seeking growth and remaining committed to and optimistic about what lies ahead.

Introduction

LEARNING TO FLY: MY MESSY LIFE AND WHY I LOVE IT

Before we dive in to all the myths we are told as women (and men, for that matter), I feel I should tell you a little more about myself—my background, my family and my career journey. By providing some context, I'll hopefully be able to bring a deeper understanding of where I come from and where the *Breaking the Glass Slipper* analysis comes from. I think I've read somewhere that "if content is king, then context is God." Let me be clear, though: You can also skip this entire chapter and head straight into the myth-busting chapters.

To give you a quick taste of my life and its chaos—uh, I mean blessings: I am a born-and-raised Texan and live in Houston. Texas comes up a lot in the book, so that's an important part of my story—typical, isn't it? We Texans always find a way to make Texas the central part of our narrative. I apologize in advance because I realize the Texas-centric mentality is super annoying for some people living outside our borders.

I've been married for 21 years to a wonderful man named Jim Turner, and we have two beautiful children together: a son named Harrison (18), and a daughter named Marlie (13). Marlie has special needs and was born with a genetic abnormality that was discovered only three years ago. Her challenging journey has shaped me in a way that words cannot do justice, and much of my soul searching has stemmed from my experience with her. I'll tell you more about her as we go along, but there are other tidbits I need to include before we get deep. Also, Jim and I jointly own a luxury lifestyle fashion business eponymously named Elaine Turner Designs. We have two adorable dogs, Brooksie and Princess (yes, you read that right—my daughter named her). And I have my parents, who live in Houston and by all accounts are kind of old, but act like they're 32. Also, I have one older brother and one older sister, who both live in Houston with their families. In other parts of the country, I have four brothers-in-law, four sisters-in-law, and 12 nieces and nephews who live in Connecticut, Minneapolis and Houston, respectively.

You see, from the outside my life looks magical, but in reality it is unbelievably complicated. In fact, I started writing several years ago at the request of my therapist to "uncomplicate" things, if you will. Journaling became a freeing and incredibly healing form of self-expression that is now a huge part of my life, along with regular date nights with Cloudy Bay Sauvignon Blanc. I know this might sound cliché (what the hell isn't anymore?), but indulge me. Over the past three or four years I've been on a journey that some would call a breakdown of sorts, but I'm choosing to see it as a spiritual awakening, a search, a renewal, a discovery . . . (see, even changing the context takes the edge off).

Ironically, at the time I met the woman I told you about in the preface, I was also at the height of my own challenges and hardship. I was in the middle of discovering more about my daughter's diagnosis and the inherent struggles she would most likely endure for the rest of her life. I could barely process anything else around me and was beginning to realize that these were not just ordinary real-life challenges. These were the type of challenges that have the potential to derail you or, worse yet, discourage you to a point of feeling hopeless. And, as any mother can imagine, when something is wrong with your baby, you will literally do anything you can to fix it. I mean anything. I'd build a f*ing rocket ship and fly around the sun 6 billion times, all while learning quantum physics (or worse, Excel), until I hear mission control say, "Houston, we DON'T have a problem" if that's what it would take to "fix" my Marlie.

To make matters worse, the hits kept coming. My mom had just finished another round of chemotherapy for a second recurrence of breast cancer and it was taking a toll on her mentally, emotionally and physically. Also, my mother-in-law suddenly and unexpectedly passed away of a stroke at the young age of 75. We witnessed the death of my 98-year-old grandfather and saw my 70-year-old uncle die a painful death from pancreatic cancer earlier that year as well.

To put it lightly, 2016 and 2017 sucked, and Jim and I were doing all we could to just hang on. So, I can safely say that all this writing really was a form of therapy for me, and at times, it felt lifesaving. Initially, I only wrote in my personal journal, and then after a while, it evolved into a blog, *Elaine's Musings*, published monthly via my company's website. Now here I am, writing a book.

For most people, when confusion and uncertainty enter their lives, a good amount of searching usually comes into play. (Don't pretend you don't WebMD your symptoms and conclude the worst.) As humans we are wired to seek answers, find truth and then set out to fix the problem. I am no different, so I set out to do what any overwhelmed, stressed-out, somewhat depressed mom would do: I started reading. I read every book on spirituality and overcoming pain and grief I could get my hands on. My bedside table started to look like the self-help section of Barnes & Noble.

And let me make this clear: I'm a communicator, so I gladly talk about what I've learned to anyone who will listen, and when I say anyone, I'm referring to my two dogs, my husband and even my 18-year-old son. I knew I had reached a low point when my son started saying things to me like "Mom, I see what you're doing here—please don't project your issues onto me." I mean, really, my son started to sound like my therapist. Shouldn't he be sneaking beer and watching a Rockets game? (Well, if I'm honest, he also does his fair share of that. He only moonlights as an adolescent therapist three times a week or so . . . . .)

Through all of this searching (psychology, Buddhism, Christianity, etc.), there was one book in particular that comforted me more than any other: *Inner Voice of Love* by Henri Nouwen, the renowned Catholic priest, writer and theologian. I actually started to take it with me everywhere I went—it was almost like a security blanket to me (better a book than pills, I guess). His words of surrender, acceptance and grace allowed me to fully embrace my challenges. In the book he says, "Because where God wants you to be, God holds you safe and gives you peace, even when there is pain." I became almost compulsive in my search for grace and continued to satiate myself with all kinds of wisdom from all kinds of sources. Oprah's *Super Soul Sunday* became a weekly Sunday afternoon ritual for me. I began reading and researching the works of Brené Brown, Elizabeth Gilbert, Anne Lamott, Richard Rohr, David Whyte, Rob Bell, Pema Chodron, Glennon Doyle Melton, Jen Hatmaker, Thomas Merton, Joseph Campbell and Eugene Peterson, to name just a few. Their books, along with many others, were safely stacked on my bedside table; I guess you could say they have become my "Soul League."

Pain Opens the Door

In my experience, the darkness is where you discover yourself. And when I say discover yourself, I mean it's in times of extreme pain that you realize just how human you really are, and with that awareness comes a humility, grace and surrender that opens us up to another way. This element of surrender can be both terrifying and liberating, yet the key to this whole pain gig is not walking away from it, but engaging with it. Don't get me wrong—a little denial never hurt anyone. But a life of denial is not a life, and usually this is where we see the divide occur. We see people either transform their pain into something that serves them or we see people become their pain and tragically slip away into a life of bitterness. I chose, and highly suggest, the former.

And the beautiful woman I told you about in the preface did, too. She chose to transform her pain into something hopeful by recognizing that she wanted to wear clothes that made her feel alive and free; free from the insidiousness of cancer.

For what it's worth, pain doesn't disappear. It might hide for a very long time, but it's always just one hurtful word, thought, slight or unexpected circumstance away. And until we walk through the "pain cloud," as I like to call it, our business here is unfinished. You have to let yourself feel the pain in order to come to terms with it and push through it. In his book *Transforming Through Pain*, Franciscan priest, author and speaker Richard Rohr writes, "Spirituality is always eventually about what you do with your pain."

I guess you could say this book is a form of transmutation of my pain and challenges, but if I'm honest with myself, it was truly born out of a deep desire to reach other women and connect through our shared wounds, our shared desires and ultimately our shared reality of attempting to do and be it all—while knowing it's an unattainable feat that most of the time leaves us feeling "less than," empty and unfulfilled.

Through all this searching, discovering and feeling painful emotions, I started accessing and allowing my God-given vulnerability, grief and compassion to flow in. It was terrifying, yet I had never felt more human.

I started to "unbecome."

As spiritual blogger and founder of momastery.com, Glennon Doyle Melton, says, "Many of us spend the first part of our adult lives *becoming*, stepping into the roles we take on so that they come to define our lives. But I've learned we don't really grow up until we *unbecome*." This is what it felt like for me. I naively thought for most of my life if I worked hard, made all the right decisions, did everything I was supposed to and flawlessly executed my many roles, then the answers would come, or better yet, success and happiness would appear. But what I didn't know then was it's never about what's to come; it's always about what is and continuing to build from there. That's where freedom is found.

Accepting the weight

So I have embarked on a new journey—a journey of acceptance. Acceptance of what is, not what should or could be. A lot like the woman in my fateful encounter, who was learning to accept her pain and dancing her way through it by allowing herself to feel beautiful. She was indulging herself and living her life instead of burying herself in grief and letting pain make her decisions.

Acceptance is hard for anyone, but it can be extremely hard for women. Women are emotionally driven, so we have our baggage (we don't travel light), plus we tend to carry the weight of everyone else's emotional baggage. Perhaps we should start charging "heavy" fees like Delta. We are built to solve, build and please, and we gladly take on the roles to prove it—mother, wife, sister, friend, volunteer, career woman, activist, artist . . . you name it, we fill it. I mean, let's get real, we are kind of a big deal. Last I knew, we do bear the responsibility of keeping the human race going. I mean, yes, men hold a vital (less painful) role in the whole deal, but we bear the responsibility of carrying and creating life. I mean, damn, we're busy. No wonder we are hard on ourselves; we all come into this life literally feeling the weight of the world on our shoulders (or, you could say, in our uteruses). It's ingrained in our primal nature to serve, and if we feel we aren't succeeding, the walls start to crumble, guilt takes over and, if we aren't careful, a downward spiral of self-criticism, resentment and bitterness sets in. Life's road has many bends, twists and curves and there is never one way to reach your destination.

The way I see it, our antidote to this ambiguous female epidemic is finding grace, peace and acceptance in one another and how we get there. Gratefully, my business has allowed me the opportunity to interact with and witness thousands of women valiantly showing up every day, fully committed to being and doing all they can to fully "become." But maybe that isn't the point; maybe we are spinning our wheels. Maybe the answer lies in "unbecoming" and allowing the layers to disappear as you discover the beauty of who you really are begin to shine through.

Speaking of my business, it plays an integral role in my life and the complication of my life. If truth be told, running a business often feels like being stuck trying to solve the most difficult *New York Times* crossword puzzle, and about 10 years into the same damn riddle, you realize that solving it might not be the point. The point might lie in the journey, showing up again and again each and every day ready to solve another clue that you pray may lead to one more right answer.

My business plays a role in who I am, who I want to be and what I want to do. Sometimes I feel like my business is a part of my family. It has kept me up at night like a newborn. It has kept me sharp, like having to answer a toddler's question about where babies come from. It has made me nervous, like watching balls hurtled at my kid on the lacrosse field. It has made me cry, like my teenager telling me they hate me. It has brought me true joy (and fear), like hanging a one-of-a-kind depiction of me looking like a Cyclops on my fridge because my kid drew it.

I love it at times. I hate it at times.

But I know without it, I'd feel incomplete. It has provided me a window into women's lives and taught me more about myself than I ever could have imagined. I started my company in 2000, and was young, naive and full of unbridled confidence and joy about launching a business. In those early days, I was solely driven by my love of design and creating beauty. To be honest, I didn't give a shit how hard it would be to make it all happen; I was determined to use the language of design to create beautiful, glamorous fashion accessories that amazing women around the world could wear and embrace.

And better yet, I was going to own my own destiny, manifest my vision and conquer the fashion industry. I had my sweet husband's support and my parents were cheering me on no matter how lofty my goals seemed.

My dad, who is my hero and inspired me to become an entrepreneur, used to say, "E, go watch, listen and learn, and then come up with your own idea and do it yourself!" SO Texan. As I reflect back now, those words spoken by my dad symbolized the oversimplifications of youth, both naïve and liberating, at once ignorant and fearless, because only youth can bring about such blind courage. Ah, to have the skin and overconfidence of a 25-year-old, and the wisdom of a 47-year-old who has been through hell and back and still believes in herself (and Botox). Inevitably though, youth fades and time marches on . . . for some slowly, and for others abruptly; we awaken to the realities of what being human or, in this instance, a woman, truly means.

By all accounts, everything looked great from the outside. I got to work with my husband. Our business was growing; we successfully opened eight stores, built a dynamic e-commerce website and launched a new personal stylist division, Elaine Turner Elite. Nonetheless, today tells a different story. The business I have poured my heart and soul into over the past 18 years is becoming harder to manage. The fashion industry has been changing at a rapid rate over the past decade and it seems to be moving faster and faster. That crossword puzzle metaphor I mentioned before only skims the surface of what running a fashion/retail business feels like nowadays. Most of the time, it feels like I'm trying to solve a new, albeit extremely difficult puzzle every single day, instead of having the chance to safely go back to the one that's already a work in progress. This creates anxiety to say the least—not having that solid foundation from which to build. Keeping up with the reality of constantly changing consumer spending habits, complete and total digital immersion in our everyday lives and a few natural disasters here and there (thanks Harvey) feels like I'm climbing Mount Kilimanjaro with no equipment, no training and no guide. I'm tired. I'm scared. I'm not in control.

Control is the key word here. Whether we want to see them or not, there are forces at work beyond our power and no matter how much hustling, working, striving and stressing I do, it's not always going to work out. There is no denying that my experiences over the last several years had already created a heightened sense of awareness within me around what it means to be human. And now my business challenges are adding fuel to the fire. It's cracked me wide open and all those scary feelings are flooding in: vulnerability, fear, sadness, grief . . . . But with this new knowledge, I have also discovered more about myself. I've started to tune in more, to listen, to take note and to trust I know more than I think I do.

Through all of this, I'm beginning to feel a dull yet persistent anxiety that seems like it is trying to tell me something. And I'm listening. As much as I love my business and design, I also realize I have a heart that is made to share, connect, inspire and ultimately help others who also might feel lost in their own unsolvable crossword puzzles. And through the significant challenges I have experienced in my life, I knew I had more to say and do and contribute. I believe I'm meant to be a mother to my daughter who desperately needs me, I believe I'm meant to continue fighting the good fight with my company and the women I serve, I believe I'm meant to write these words for others to read and benefit from . . . It feels like a gravitational pull toward becoming who I really am, not who I feel I should be. In essence, I felt called to be a cheerleader for all women, one who can help you adjust your crown without ever making you feel like it was crooked to begin with.

So, here we are. This book is a culmination of goose-bump fate, setbacks, hard truths, courage, empowering optimism, acceptance and heart. It is about letting go of fear, failure and expectations. It is about realizing we don't have to fit a mold and we don't have to be a victim to our struggles. It's about shattering the myths you have been told, sold and programmed to believe, and ultimately, it's about finding your own truth. A truth that keeps you from ever needing a glass slipper—because why walk when truth lets you fly?

* * *

Chapter 1

MYTH: FASHION IS FRIVOLOUS

Michael Jackson, Pirate Shirts and a Love Child

I have this theory that people think fashion is frivolous because they don't understand it outside of the concept of utility. Maybe it's that there is no science to it? Maybe it's that it invites fantasy into reality? Maybe it's because its cyclical and fleeting nature makes it seem impossible to keep up with, almost unstable and untouchable? The truth of it is fashion touches all of us, even if we don't realize it. It's this magical place where your right brain and left brain collide in a cosmic way. It can speak for you, carry you through life transitions and comfort you in a way only a worn-in set of college sweats can after a long Spanx squeeze.

Speaking of sweats, I asked a woman whose version of sweats is a cashmere sweater set (my mom) to recall the first moment she knew I was destined for a fashion future.

"Elaine had just turned six years old and was beginning the first grade. I had made it my habit to set her clothes out the night before so there wouldn't be a delay getting ready for school the next morning. One night she asked if she could put together her own outfit because she had been thinking about how much fun that would be. I agreed, and later, after she was asleep, I checked out what she had selected.

"It wasn't entirely appropriate for school, but it was her decision and I knew it was important to her. She had laid out a full-length green velvet jumper-type dress and a white blouse with very large puffy pirate-type sleeves to wear under it. Elaine put it on the next morning and was beaming with pride. As I watched her walk down the stairs that morning in a bright green velvet jumper with white patent leather boots, looking like Michael Jackson, I knew fashion was on her horizon. I could tell Elaine got lots of attention from teachers and friends on her outfit that day. From then on, Elaine had a big say in what she was going to wear and I recognized that putting outfits together was obviously her creative way of expressing herself. It was at that same age that Elaine began to be very aware of fashion and fashion trends. I still remember how proud she was of her rainbow collection of Gloria Vanderbilt jeans. She literally had every single color."

Thank God for "blind love" because my chic mother let me leave the house looking like I was some sort of weird love child of the Jackson 5 and Captain & Tennille. I'd insert a picture, but I reserve the right to protect myself from providing Google-able content from back when Google wasn't around to dig up scary skeletons.

Love child aside, the ability to leave the house in whatever statement I wanted to make helped me find the ultimate freedom. A freedom that's found not after a rite of passage, but from making choices for myself, both good and bad. A freedom that gave me words when I couldn't find my own. A freedom that gave me confidence when I hit puberty and confidence was hard to find. A freedom that made me believe I could be a member of the Jackson 5 if I damn well pleased. That freedom is worth every cringe-worthy photo and polyester pit stain I ever endured.

Every Designer Needs a Muse

For as long as I can remember, I've been drawn to fashion, and can't recall a time when it wasn't a part of my life in some capacity. Some of my earliest memories are when I was four or five years old; I was always in my mom's closet trying on clothes, shoes and handbags to see what magical (or at least what I thought was magical) outfit I could create. I was in awe of her and her style. She had a refined, ladylike sensibility, but wasn't afraid to update her look with something unexpected. When I think of my mom, I have this time-capsule image of her wearing a gold trench coat, oversized tortoise-rimmed sunglasses and an opal choker with her thick, chestnut Farrah Fawcett hairstyle perfectly coiffed. She epitomized 1970s glamour. (Faye Dunaway who?) She was and is my muse, and I attribute my mother's effortlessly glamorous style to the brand I have created today. My mom was ahead of her time in fashion and in motherhood, too. In a culture that celebrates left-brain achievements, she was celebrating my right-brain creativity and never forcing me to be anyone other than my truest self.

She is responsible for getting me into fashion and she loved fashion, too, so I naturally learned a lot from her. My mom honored fashion as an art form, and instilled in me the concept that fashion is a mode of self-expression. She would often say it was our "visual language to the world." I'll never forget the impact those words had on me; it planted a seed of confidence in me that I might not have otherwise received.

See, I was kind of polarized. I was a tomboy, but also drawn to communicating through my clothes, jewelry and hair (I'm a Leo, so my hair is always a "mane event"). I had a masculine interior and could hold my own with the boys, but I never missed an opportunity to glam up and head to the mall with my girlfriends. As I got older, I really came into the feminine side of my body and psyche, but I still held onto my tomboy strength. My mom tapped into that—she really got it. And thank God she did, because without her support and encouragement I'm not sure I would have had the courage to build a career in fashion. Her words left a huge impact on me and created lasting positive memories that I'm sure led me on my fashion journey.

It's a good reminder for me to recognize and remember the power of my words, especially as I raise my own children. "Be mindful of the words you choose; a string of words that don't mean much to you may stick with someone else a lifetime," says author Rachel Wolchin. Fortunately, my mom's words were supportive and reinforcing, even if my passions weren't what society deemed important. She was always telling me, "E, I love that! How did you put that together?" Sometimes all it takes is one person saying something point-blank for it to register.

Having someone believe in your capabilities and talents often leads to further curiosity and exploration of the thing you love. It also inspires you to share what you love with others. I think this has been the case with me. My mom told me I was good at fashion and everything took off from there.

Decades later, with my own business, I've seen the power of collaboration—what can happen when a group of like-minded people come together to create. It triggers a communal, collaborative process—a process of exploration, back-and-forth brainstorming and idea creation. To this day, I can still sit for hours with my design team analyzing the latest trends and looking at color palettes, leathers and textiles. There's a freedom in letting go of the rules and coloring outside the lines as a team. I like to call it divergent thinking. And in my eyes, divergent thinking is the backbone of creativity. It leads to a better understanding of what is and then imagining the possibilities of what could be. Some say tapping into your creativity leads to your higher self. Some say creativity and spirituality are two sides of the same coin; that safe, soothing place where your mind stops racing and time seems to stop. Some call this flow, enlightenment or "the zone." Whatever it is—I want more of it.

Let's go deeper and explore the myth that fashion is frivolous, materialistic and only for a select few.

Finding Freedom in Fashion

Fashion has gotten a bad rap. Huge movements toward "minimalism" and "essentialism" have intensified questions about fashion's ubiquity, vanity and unimportance. The myth is that it's superficial and that you have to be a certain body type, have a bunch of money and have to struggle to "find your own sense of style."

To be honest, style has nothing to do with the clothes on your back. Style is all about how you carry yourself and project yourself to the world. More than what you're wearing, it's about an overall attitude and sense of ease with yourself. It's never about carrying the latest Birkin bag or wearing the newest Cartier watch, because—let's get real for a moment—the things you own actually own you. It's a slippery slope to fall into the idea that you need *things* to fulfill you; you'll soon find you don't feel free at all. You actually feel chained to your "stuff." Both men and women tend to think, "If I have *X*, my life will be better." But the truth is it will only be enough for so long; soon we will want more. The "it" bag will only be "it" for so long. The raise will only be "plenty of money" for so long.

The things we have don't define us. There's a saying that goes "You will never find true love until you love yourself." Same goes for fashion. It takes time to develop a fashion relationship with yourself, where you are wearing the clothes and they aren't wearing you. It takes experimenting, playing, finding your balance and choosing pieces that enhance what you already have RIGHT NOW, not the things or body you idealize. Having a true sense of style and fashion is deeper than that. It's a feeling. A feeling that you own who you are and are comfortable in your own skin. With this freedom comes fearlessness, and with that comes a true acceptance of who you are at that very moment.

In today's world, there's so much pressure to define and edit yourself to a T. Our identities cannot be defined by one particular style, iPhone picture or cleverly curated Instagram post. Our identities aren't set in stone and neither is our sense of style. We grow, evolve, change. Yeah, we all have throwback playlists we'd be embarrassed if the valet guy heard, but all of these preferences over time help tell a story only you can tell. We have different moods on different days and go through peaks of confidence and valleys of self-doubt. And guess what? That's OK. It's OK to be exactly who you are and to feel exactly how you feel.

You know what's not OK? Constantly editing yourself or aspiring to some idea of a picture-perfect, untouchable version of yourself. Snoozeville. At Elaine Turner, we are about fun, freedom and effortless style. We exist to enhance your already perfectly imperfect self. My true joy is finding beauty in what's real and being OK with yourself today, not dwelling in the past or fretting about the future. We are about having fun, being nice and knowing a laugh (or snort) begets a laugh (or a snort, or worse, a fart). So say goodbye to faking it and hello to owning it. Free yourself from the shackles of expectations you and society have, and explore the greatness you already have within by finding your own unique sense of style.

The Great Communicator

We spend most of our lives trying to understand and to be understood. For instance, I want my children to understand that I am sometimes the Queen Bee, so I communicate in a British accent and ask them to call me Kate... although having them call me Meghan would take a lot of pressure off a perfect British accent. (Now, how's that for a breakthrough?!) From fascinators to jeans and a T-shirt, clothing is one of the major ways of revealing who we are to others. In this respect, clothing is actually a form of communication.

We may not realize it, but the way we dress gives everyone around us all kinds of information about who we are. If you're someone who wears a lot of black, your no-nonsense approach to dressing might convey how you approach life in general. If you love busy prints and bright colors, you might not be afraid to take risks or be different. Through the clothes we wear, the bags we carry and the jewelry we put on, we are expressing hundreds of things about ourselves without even opening our mouths.

For instance, I tend to go for more ladylike glamour and love caftans, bold jewelry and stiletto heels. My sister, Valerie, on the other hand, is the complete opposite (it's amazing we were raised in the same family). Growing up with my mom and me, I think she was always questioning herself—"I don't know if that's who I am"—but she tried. She tried to do the beaded cocktail dress thing with us, but it just wasn't her. Years later, and I think it might have come from listening to me, she has come into her own and has started to embrace her style. She prefers bohemian-inspired designs and is very practical. What I love about it is the latest or overly priced designer clothes are not important to Valerie. Her style is about honoring herself and who she really is. That's what is beautiful. She's dressing in a way that brings her comfort and makes her feel true to herself. Maybe the result is a pair of Birkenstocks, a high quality T-shirt and a cute pair of well-fit jeans, but the important thing is staying true to who you are.

Throughout my career, I have heard a lot of people say they're "too lazy" to be fashionable or "I'm just not into fashion." I've started to understand that this is usually code for "fashion makes me insecure." Maybe it's not where your confidence is and you think *I just can't do it,* but my hope is that I can help. If only I could invent a Myers-Briggs fashion personality test to make finding your place in fashion as simple as an acronym . . . but there we go again trying to make fashion a science.

One of my dear friends always insisted she was NOT INTO FASHION, which made me question if we should be friends at all. (Kidding!) I kept encouraging her to stop by one of our stores and to keep an open mind about it all. Well, to this day, I still have the voicemail she left me. This is what she said: "E, you were right. I walked in there and they allowed me to be myself; they listened to me and understood my lifestyle. I told them I am a jeans-and–T-shirt kind of gal and they brought me options to simply enhance what I already owned. They encouraged me to try on some fun, easy dresses, too, that I would have normally not tried on. I walked out of there feeling like a million bucks. Thanks for pushing me over the edge!"

These are the stories that get me up in the morning. Another illustration of witnessing a fashion epiphany was watching my former EVP, over the course of a decade, evolve from an anti-fashion, casual, athletic woman into a gorgeous fashion plate. It was profound. Her expression was a pencil skirt and cute jacket, and in those pieces she became an absolute powerhouse. I watched her transform before my eyes and discover what works for her, her body and her lifestyle.

The Darker Side of Fashion

Come to the dark side with me for a bit. I want to recognize that our society sometimes perpetuates the notion that if you're attached to the fashion world, you're somehow lacking depth, emotionally or intellectually. I think this stems from a very real truth. The reality is, we are bombarded with images in today's world of over-the-top pop-culture icons, unrealistic social media imagery and relentless advertising pulpits preaching to us 24/7 that "you need more, you must have more!" We are living in a "faster is better" society. Fast fashion has taken over the industry and made it almost impossible to compete on quality or price. We have our so-called fashion icons showing off their latest fashion finds and showcasing them like it's some sort of silly, expensive hobby.

But for most of us, I think we just want to feel good in our own skin and enjoy what fashion can offer us. If truth be told, when I reflect on the actualization of my dreams-to-reality story, it's not as cut and dried as it may seem. In college, I was actually embarrassed about my dream to go into fashion. I never denied my passion for sartorial expression, but in a self-deprecating way, I always joked about my silly interest for clothing. I thought my zeal for style was superficial, so instead of pursuing fashion, I pursued advertising (and in hindsight, that might not have been much better!).

Some could argue the idea of fashion being vacuous or shallow goes back to its original purpose of declaring our "class" status to others. Back in the 19th century, for instance, high-class women were programmed to wear pinnings, corsets and even hobble skirts and undergarments. These clothes were designed with the intent to impede one from "working," therefore showcasing their place in society. Fashion became aligned with socioeconomic divide and deep materialism. And when the 1960s rolled around, the message of the day was anti-establishment. It all became a bit negative. And, the excess of the '80s didn't help much either: big hair, big shoulder pads, big money (and even bigger fashion regrets). It was all about how much we could consume. So, yes, like most things in life the good comes with the bad. When our fashion choices come from a place of truth and authenticity it just feels better.

Life's Big Fashion Moments

Most of us, no matter how fashion savvy, don't realize just how much fashion carries us through big moments in our lives: graduation gowns, wedding gowns, first power suit, maternity clothes, nursing tops (where were those for all my postpartum nip slips?!), mom jeans, etc. Fashion plays a huge role in so many of life's big moments or transitions and we often forget just how defining those fashion choices are to our memories. These fashion choices make important memories seem more tangible. I think fashion sense is almost as powerful as the sense of smell. Remembering exactly what you were wearing can put you right back in that moment again. It's pretty damn powerful if you think about it. Should we have a moment of silence here?

In all seriousness, it's really interesting: The big events tend to bring out other sides of people, sides that really aren't necessarily them when they think they've worn something so out of character. I certainly did that. For instance, one year my mom took me to Sakowitz, a high-end, family-run specialty store in Houston, for my prom dress. I chose a long black strapless gown with a large white ruffle peplum in the midsection, and I wore long white gloves. I thought I was a mother f*ing star! I looked so good. Now I look back and think, *Oh my gosh, what was I thinking?!* The contrast of the black and white with the full-on white ruffle peplum wouldn't work on my well-aged body now. Ay yai yai!!

And the memorable fashion choices don't end there. Jim and I got engaged in New York, and buying my dress was geared toward the outdoor garden wedding we were planning. For some reason, I had my heart set on having a romantic, dreamy European-inspired wedding, even though I was marrying a Midwestern, all-American boy. Oh well, a girl can dream . . . My mom and sister came with me to Saks, where I found a Lazaro dress with a fitted silk satin tank bodice and full tulle lace skirt. I felt like a Spanish princess, and to be honest, that is 100 percent what I wanted to feel like. I have good memories of that process, but I do know that shopping for a wedding dress can make you feel vulnerable. Everybody builds it up to be this super-important thing and you feel you have to look perfect. You try on dresses and people critique you. I remember getting my feelings hurt a little when my mom said my arms looked too thick for the sleeveless Lazaro dress. But the saleslady said, “Oh no, ma’am, I don’t think you’re right telling her that.” I had accepted my mom’s comment without question, but then I stopped and said, “You know what? I’m over it. I’m wearing the sleeveless dress.” You see, even in a moment of self doubt, the fashion choices we make can empower us to embrace who we are and who we want to be in any given moment.

Fashion Icons: Good and Bad

Admiring fashionable people is a way to learn and be inspired, but as we all know, there can be a downside to having icons. We respect strong, smart, ambitious, kick-ass women and want our children to do so as well. So what’s with all the sexy, pouty, famous-for-being-famous and getting-by-on-looks-alone female celebrities? It has gotten so much worse with Instagram, which is all about carefully curated images. The 24/7 unrealistic imagery, always flashing and inundating our already overloaded senses. There is so much illusion that we need to offset... It’s exhausting.

However, there are some good ones too. Coco Chanel introduced a more relaxed way of dressing—no corsets—and set the stage for modern dressing today. I guess if I had to list some of my more current icons, I'd put Carolyn Bessette-Kennedy at the top of the list. She had a huge impact on fashion with her refined yet effortless appeal. Everything she wore was simple and classic: black or white with simple lines, but she always made it look fresh, edgy and modern. She exuded individuality. I'm also loving the modern royals, Kate Middleton and Meghan Markle, who are remaining true to their style while under a microscope. They are two beautiful women who take so much pride in dressing well. This may surprise you, but I also love Pink and Lady Gaga because they are so irreverent and FREE. And India Hicks' relaxed island lifestyle has had a huge influence on me. (Okay maybe more than influenced me—I kinda want her life!)

When cultivating my brand, I referenced my list of past and present icons (weird how I can make an icon list, yet making a grocery list is completely lost on me). With strong footing in my own style and a collection of style icons, I founded my company's DNA in classic beauties such as Grace Kelly and Katharine Hepburn. (Who would have thought I'd go from Michael Jackson to Grace Kelly? See, you do evolve, thank God!) Jackie O's effortless style also helped lay the groundwork for my company's sensibility; she could go from a Chanel suit to preppy corduroys and own any style, dressy or casual, so quickly.

All of the women I mentioned above had one thing in common—individuality. It goes without saying that each one of them possessed the allure of Old Hollywood Glamour and timeless classicism, yet they all interpreted it in their own way. Grace Kelly's namesake "Kelly" bag, signature pearls and cinched in waist; Katherine Hepburn's ground breaking pants and masculine meets feminine vibe, and Jackie O's relaxed, modern femininity where white gloves and iconic round sunglasses completed most of her looks. All of these women set the stage for what so many of us aspire to be today. They were not only fearless, they were authentic. And for that I am thankful because it laid the foundation for what I've built today.

What I Stand For (Fashionably Speaking)

I take great pride in the responsibility I have to project self-acceptance, positivity and fun into the world. For me that starts with how I size my clothes. I'm staying true to my values by offering easy silhouettes that are flattering, look polished and fit most body types. I started designing apparel about three years ago and from day one, I was adamant that the pieces I design fit a wide range of shapes and sizes. This is why all of my apparel is sized XS-XL. There is built in wiggle room across all sizes and nothing comes down to a matter of centimeters or inches to bump you up or down a size. If you are normally a size 8—you might very well be a size small at Elaine Turner. I don't want women to feel like their body size is associated with a number—the lower the number, the smaller you are—the higher the number, the larger you are. HOGWASH. A woman's body transcends a number. And, your body is yours alone to be celebrated as beautiful, strong and unique.

I'm acutely aware that young girls will see my images whether it be on my social media feed or my ecommerce site. And, as I stated before, most young people today are bombarded with 24/7 round the clock imagery that is filled with unrealistic standards. It's natural to look for role models as we scour through endless images hoping to find similarities with other people. Aren't we all in search of feeling less alone and more understood? When we feel like we can relate to others, we feel a deeper understanding with ourselves and those around us.

The biggest differences I see today from when I grew up are simple: time and space. The time and space to just process the information and imagery coming at you. The simple act of 'being' seems to be slowly dying. Sitting still and allowing more time to process allows us to turn inward and understand what feels right and what doesn't. Just think of what could happen if young people felt empowered to question the imagery that incessantly invades their iPhones. What if they stopped to ask themselves the hard questions when something doesn't feel right; an overly thin model, a sexually gratuitous or exploitive photo. By doing this, you build the confidence that you can make decisions that feel right for you and break the perpetuation of negative imagery. As Gandhi says, "Be the change you wish to see in the world." I want to encourage people to question the images they see and to have icons that they can relate to, so, I'm sensitive about what I project through my company, that it not lead to making people feel "less than."

I am also passionate about finding out what you're comfortable wearing. Are you a jeans and classic white button-down kinda girl? Great! Let's start there. I preach to all my team members that our company does not exist to change a woman's style; we exist to ENHANCE a woman's style. At Elaine Turner we aim to fill in the gaps and hopefully add some core pieces to your wardrobe that complete your outfit or look. I strive to educate my customers on how they can incorporate items into their closet that are versatile and function for them in their everyday lives. We focus on travel-friendly, easy care garments and multipurpose handbags that can take you from day to night with ease. It's all about that "aha moment" when a beautiful woman is standing in front of me and says, "Oh, I can do that," and she realizes she can be a little more than she originally thought she could be. Sometimes we get so wrapped up in untouchable icons that we forget we can create our own iconic looks that work for our life. Fashion is transformative and powerful if we embrace it as our truest, most authentic self.

At its best, fashion has the ability to create an emotional experience that opens a window into who you could become. It has the potential to shine a light on the very best part of you. Like the story I told you in the preface about the terminally ill woman who came to my store after seeing my collection on TV that morning—fashion is emotional. It taps into your feelings. Ultimately, I want women to feel beautiful inside and out when they experience my brand. I want the products to evoke a sense of fantasy, happiness and wanderlust. For the woman I met, the vibrant colors, glamorous silhouettes and bold accessories all evoked a sense of escapism for her. It gave her an opportunity to be swept away, and if only for a few minutes or hours, possibly forget about her ailing health and enjoy what it feels like to be fully alive and wrapped in beauty.

ASK YOURSELF

Fashion can be an artistic and fun experience. If that's a new concept to you, there might be some anxiety attached. See if you can find the freedom to discover more about yourself, your limits and your comfort zone. Answer these prompts:

1. **Think back.** Do you remember a time when you wore an outfit that made you feel comfortable, free and happy? What made you feel so good about it? It's time you got back to that. Do you love wearing sweaters? Find dresses and other pieces that give you that same cozy but pulled-together feeling. Choose fabrics that have a warm, soft hand

and move easily with the body. There are always fabric and silhouette options available to help you replicate what you know makes you feel good.

2. **Simplify.** Lots of us have too many clothes. We really don't need to accumulate so much. Find pieces you love and wear them often instead of buying more (you might want to show this to your husband—or not). If a piece is pricier than you're used to, do a CPW (cost per wear) calculation, and it might be worth it. Buy well instead of buying more. Look for pieces that will take you into many parts of your life. That's something we pride ourselves in at Elaine Turner—showing our clients seven core pieces and how to build on them. Showing you a little black dress and a bomber jacket, and how you can be set for days.
3. **Shop your closet.** Here's a twist on the "tidying up" concept: Put away things you love now, then go back to them in a few months. Maybe you've collected pieces over 25 years that you can revisit and be delighted with again. I have a Donna Karan leather blazer that I spent a fortune on, and I'll never give it up. If it brings you joy, don't part with it. Don't be afraid to cherish something: your grandmother's stole, Aunt Grace's spectator Ferragamos. If it makes you happy, wear it.
4. **Emotions and shopping.** Tune in and explore your feelings around shopping. See what pops

up. This simple exercise can bring awareness to negative thoughts and emotions around buying clothes. What emotions do you feel when you buy clothes (unhappy, angry, depressed, jealous, guilty, defeated, poor, lonely, annoyed, sad, frustrated, etc.)? What circumstance or event just occurred (promotion, illness, birthday/celebration, loss of relationship, fight/disagreement, loss of job, just got paid, rejected over something you thought you deserved, receiving something you feel you didn't deserve, etc.)? How soon did you wear the garment after buying?

* * *

Chapter 2

THE CINDERELLA MYTH

How Far Will We Go to Fit Into That Glass Slipper?

We learn so many things from the fairy tales we hear as children, as little girls. *Cinderella* is the most influential, of course, along with *Snow White and the Seven Dwarfs*. We learn what a woman is supposed to be from the images we see and the stories we hear. We learn that if we align ourselves with the right man and have babies, everything will work out. It doesn't, of course. Those lessons are dangerous and I believe hold us back. They certainly had that effect on me. Thankfully, today we have come a long way with our fairy tales. *Frozen* was particularly refreshing with its celebration of sisterly love and strong female protagonists. And *The Princess and The Frog* shattered stereotypes by showcasing the first African American princess who was both resourceful and ambitious, and she was NOT saved by a prince! Hallelujah!

As we all know, Cinderella was the victim of a miserable set of circumstances. Her beloved mother died and her father all but abandoned her—first by marrying a wretched woman, then by dying himself and leaving her in her stepmother's care. When a local prince declares he is looking for a princess, the claws come all the way out: The stepmother wants one of her two daughters to snag the prince (I always wondered what would happen to the other one!) and works tirelessly to not only push her girls to the forefront, but also to deny Cinderella any chance of success.

Poor Cinderella doesn't have anything to wear—and, of course, looking beautiful is the most important attribute a woman can possess, especially if she wants to nab a prince. So, the Disney version of Cinderella gives her some mice and birds to help her build a beautiful dress, which her stepsisters tear to shreds. Poor Cinderella! She is saved by her pudgy, motherly fairy godmother, who creates the most fabulous dress in the world, along with a pair of almost magical glass slippers.

Well, it all worked, and we know the rest of the story. There have been nearly 700 versions of it told through the ages and across the world, including a brutal tale by the Brothers Grimm. In that version, the stepsisters mutilate their feet in order to fit into the slippers, illustrating that women will go to ghastly lengths to thwart their rivals. Russian czars were known for holding these kinds of mass auditions when they needed a new princess. Beautiful peasant girls were brought by their families to be seen, and with any luck, chosen by the czar. Not only did the winner become an instant royal, but her family never saw hardship again. If everything went well, that is. You can even find a definition of "Cinderella" in the dictionary:

"One resembling the fairy-tale Cinderella. One suddenly lifted from obscurity and neglect to a place of honor or significance; someone or something previously unknown or given little attention, and suddenly successful."

And here's the thing: In the fairy tales, including movies such as *Splash* and *Pretty Woman*, the "Cinderellas" are always female and always pretty helpless. In fact, in the most popular Cinderella movie, Disney's 1950 version, our heroine is the most passive. Not only do these stories encourage women to be passive, but they also pit women against each other, since there are only so many powerful (and rich) men to go around. They lead us to attach ourselves to men (bosses, teammates, co-workers) even if they aren't our mates. And while there might be plenty of that most important fairy tale attribute—beauty—out there, beauty is so subjective that it's a much less tangible achievement than a dream or kick-ass job or a thriving business.

Even successful, beloved celebrities battle with perpetuating the Cinderella myth. Recently Amy Zimmerman wrote in *The Daily Beast* about the media obsession with Jennifer Aniston's struggle to have children, and the widespread assertion that her "barrenness" is the reason for her split with Justin Theroux. Zimmerman quotes a piece Aniston wrote for *The Huffington Post* stating that while she wasn't pregnant, she was fed up. "I'm fed up with the sport-like scrutiny and body shaming that occurs daily under the guise of 'journalism,' the 'First

Amendment' and 'celebrity news,'" Aniston proclaimed. "The sheer amount of resources being spent right now by press trying to simply uncover whether or not I am pregnant (for the bajillionth time . . . but who's counting) points to the perpetuation of this notion that women are somehow incomplete, unsuccessful or unhappy if they're not married with children." Aniston is just one more reminder that society has tied our value as women to our womb and our wedding ring, making her seem helpless or unappealing for "failing" at her womanly roles.

I want to go deeper with you on why as women we tend to believe these myths: that if I'm nice, pretty, polite, gracious and hardworking, justice will most certainly prevail or, better yet, I will be saved. Let's explore the themes of beauty, male dependency and gender roles and the effects they have on us.

Because, let's face it, gender roles cut you off at the foot—so there goes that glass slipper.

Mirror Mirror on the Wall, Who's the Fairest of Them All?

The doorbell rang. I remember my mom and dad talking to my swim coaches about taking me to train at a highly competitive Amateur Athletic Union training center. I had gotten into swimming competitively around the age of seven, and I quickly became one of the best swimmers on my neighborhood team and was winning swim meets in our region. I was up in my room waiting anxiously for my mom to call me downstairs, but that never happened. After about 45 minutes, my mom came upstairs and into my bedroom. I was sitting on my bed and she said she wanted to talk to me. I was only seven or eight years old at the time and I remember feeling confused as to what she was going to tell me. She sat down next to me and told me she was concerned if I continued swimming at such a competitive level that I might start looking like a boy. She went on to say, "Your neck will get thicker and your back and arms will get bigger." It quickly dawned on me that my mom was afraid that I might not be accepted as a lady. This is the first time I ever remember thinking about my gender and the appearance associated with it, which led to an onslaught of anxiety and inner turmoil.

You have to understand: I was the girl who arm-wrestled the boys. I was strong and athletic and not ashamed of it. I held my own with boys in bravado and I could swear better than Tom, Harry and Dick combined (still can). But for me, the recognition that I'd lose my feminine edge if I continued competing was a big turning point and I quit swimming because of it. When I stopped swimming, I started playing tennis. And then, at 14, I gravitated away from tennis because I wanted to cultivate my social skills and experiment with having more friends, which I saw as more feminine. I knew I didn't want to make a career of athletics, so I came into young adulthood manifesting more of my social and creative sides. And

I guess I haven't looked back. Even though I turned my interest toward more inherently "feminine" aspects of my soul, I never lost the strength and not-always-graceful athleticism because, to be honest, they are innately a part of me . . . and there was a hole in the ceiling at my University of Texas sorority house to prove it. We were in the middle of UT rush and we were all screaming and jumping on a table, and my head and arms went through the ceiling. Long story, but yes, you can assume swear words were used . . . loudly.

I don't blame my mother, or any of our mothers; they were from a generation that was not given as many opportunities or choices to become independent and successful without having to attach themselves to a man or use their feminine finesse to define their roles. Everyone is (and was) doing the best they can do with what they are given. There are so many factors that come into play on how our mothers raised us: timing, programming, societal messages, politics, etc. It's complicated. In my mother's case, I think she was influenced more by society and her natural feminine predisposition and tendencies than her own mother's beliefs about women and how they should look and act. My grandmother was one of a kind and way ahead of her time; more on her later.

I wasn't obsessed with Barbie nor did I wear princess costumes. I was a tomboy at heart and my mom was the quintessential lady. I guess you could say I not only got the message that I couldn't be good enough on my own from toys and movies and TV cartoons, but I also had a mother whose programming and innate female persona was different from mine. She exuded beauty, polish and femininity. I, on the other hand, was competing with the boys in the pool and on the tennis court, and I had the biceps to prove it.

Let me make this clear: My mom was and is an incredibly progressive person; I don't think she ever intended to create a shred of insecurity in me. She honored me and who I was, yet we were two very different people. I give her credit for getting me into tennis and swimming at such a young age. Mom intuitively knew I needed physical outlets. I remember her bringing home my first tennis racquet (a red-rimmed aluminum Head racquet, if you must know), and if style could score me points, I would have hit an ace in record time. However, I do think there was some inherent frustration because she probably couldn't quite relate to me.

Thank goodness, five or six years ago I got back in touch with my physical side when I discovered yoga. When I was a kid, my coaches would always say, "You know, for a girl, you are really strong." Now my yoga teachers say, "You know, you're not that flexible, but you are really strong." When I'm doing yoga, I find myself manifesting grace, ease and mindfulness, all while finding the physical strength to hold a pose. Yoga is a beautiful, metaphorical dance between the masculine and feminine. Or some might say it creates an awareness around the dualities of life: yin and yang, dark and light. In yoga, every pose has a countermovement, and this must be essential in how yoga shapes the heart and mind, knowing that every action has an opposing action and that happy will also be met with sad, and in turn sad will also be met with happy. It brings a clarity and acceptance to the sacred center of NOW and fully and abidingly living there always.

I think most women struggle trying to balance our feminine and masculine qualities. It's encouraging and inspiring to see gender roles start to work their way into the past, but what about gender energy? We all have both energies at work inside of us and we must welcome the balancing act of both. Society has separated the two for thousands of years without much discussion on how we should navigate and balance both sides. I do feel we are in an extremely important time for humanity. Feminine qualities are getting more praise and attention; however, we must be careful to not shun or demonize the masculine in order to bring more power to the feminine.

I am in a constant battle with this in my own life. My company is all about pink and femininity, but my innate personality is also very masculine. When I was growing up, everyone always told me I was a lot like my dad. He has a crazy sense of humor and cusses a lot, and to my mother's dismay, so do I. I would never describe myself as a girly girl, yet my feminine side is very much an aspect of who I am as well. I think being raised by two strong parents—one who was highly feminine and the other strongly masculine—set an example of how both energies are fully expressed. Throughout my life, I have nurtured and developed my masculine and feminine sides at certain times to varying degrees. For example, in my company, I see my masculine side take hold through my take-charge mentality, my passion for entrepreneurism and my tendency toward taking risks. Conversely, I embrace my feminine side through my intuition, compassion and creativity. It sounds so cliché, but it's about trying to find the balance of the two (key word *trying*), and in doing so, we can strengthen our self-awareness and the relationships around us and hopefully reach a place of peace.

Speaking of feminine versus masculine, another thing that continues to gnaw at me is where is Cinderella's anger? Why isn't Cinderella putting up a fight? Why isn't she cursing (even under her breath)? Why isn't she letting herself be heard? Apart from passivity and the physical danger of trying to acquire that tiny waist, the fairy tales also set up the dichotomy of having to be the princess—passive and kind—who never gets angry. No one talks about owning our anger better than Anne Lamott. In *Bird by Bird: Some Instructions on Writing and Life,* she writes, "You can't get to any of these truths by sitting in a field smiling beatifically, avoiding your anger and damage and grief. Your anger and damage and grief are the way to the truth." We often regard angry feelings as negative (or, dare I say, overly masculine) because anger can be connected with aggression. Yet, when we bring a sense of awareness around our anger, it can bring attention to a problem in our life that needs to be addressed, and this, my friends, can move us toward healing. We need to be OK expressing our full set of emotions, and owning our humanness, and never apologizing for allowing ourselves to *feel*.

Let's not get stuck being silent and kind. We don't have to be the victim waiting to be saved and believing that the only real love is love at first sight, or love that rides in on a horse to save us. I believe you can change the circumstances of your life; you don't need a man or even a fairy godmother. You can find that courage within yourself. Outside answers are fleeting and typically expire at midnight (like most good sales).

You Are the Answer

Like most people from Texas, I love Texas. The independent, can-do spirit is infectious. And honestly, you can't beat the people. I was born and bred in Houston and have watched this city grow from being an oil boom (or bust) town to a multiculturally diverse city with economic diversification and prosperity. But underlying the light is the darkness. As much as Texas has evolved, a machismo mentality can still be felt and seen. There are women here who find their identity by attaching themselves to a man: his income, his power and his stuff. Their identities are completely aligned with the man they married. They are perfectly capable and educated, but they exhibit that helplessness. And then, if they get divorced (because shit happens), many women don't believe they can figure it out on their own; they think they have to find someone else who can take care of them financially. It's all about looking for someone to save them. Thanks, Cinderella.

It's funny, I look at my mom and what society was telling her in the late '50s and early '60s: "Not to be rude, but your education isn't as important as you think it is; you just have to find the right man." But she knew better. She taught my sister and me that we needed an education and to be self-reliant. And when she hit middle age and all her kids went to college, she found her voice and started her own publishing company. I watched it all happen and was in awe of her. She showed me that no matter who you are, it's never too late. Your dreams are there no matter what phase of life you're in.

We get stuck thinking we have to follow society's elusive timeline for success: We get married in our 20s, build our career in our 30s and 40s, and pretty much hang it up in our 50s and 60s. I call bullshit on that timeline, and I have my mom to thank for that. If truth be told, Mom was somewhat hidden under the responsibilities of motherhood and wife for so many years, but then was able to find her voice and accept herself and soar! Also, my grandmother was a huge source of inspiration for me. She was a rock. She raised her three kids in an era when women had one role: to stay at home and raise the kids.

Period. My grandfather worked overseas on oil barges and was gone for most of my mother's childhood. Mom tells us stories about my grandmother making ends meet and juggling it all on her own. She paved the way for me to believe I could also be or do anything I wanted to.

And last, but not least, my best friend Rebecca is a single mother. She has been divorced for more than 16 years and raised her kids on her own. She talks about how tempted she was to remarry and depend on someone to help her, yet she tells me something inside of her told her to put her kids first and do it on her own. I often think about her children and what they have seen their mom do. I wonder how it will shape their lives. Her kids are now 18 and heading off to college soon, and I see her already opening up to what the next chapter will bring. I won't be surprised if she finds love again, but I guess she needed to do it in her own time and way. The self-reliance, independence and ultimate self-empowerment of knowing you can and will survive is essential in our ability to see ourselves as enough. What could possibly be more liberating than that?

We've Come a Long Way, but Not Far Enough Yet

And another thing: Until women believe we are enough, the message of needing to be saved is not going away. We aren't there yet. Which, to me, to be quite frank, is shocking. The truth is, we as a society are not ready to elect a woman president, no matter what other reasons we come up with.

Not so in many other countries. Indira Gandhi ruled India as prime minister for 11 years, 1966 to 1977, and then again for nearly five more years in the 1980s. Golda Meir was prime minister of Israel from 1970 to 1977, and Margaret Thatcher of England for nearly 12 years. Corazon Aquino led the Philippines as president, 1986 though 1992. Prime ministers Theresa May of Great Britain and Jacinda Ardern of New Zealand are still holding strong. And Angela Merkel has been head of state as chancellor of Germany since 2005.

As close as we came, there has not yet been a female president of the United States. In fact, we are still woefully underrepresented. Since the establishment of the U.S. Senate in 1789, just 51 women have been elected to that branch of government. Currently there are 22 female senators out of 100. And some states have not yet elected a woman to the Senate. The House of Representatives was also founded in 1789, and so far almost 300 women have served; as of June 2017, there are 84 women in the House. As of 2009, only 12 Fortune 500 companies and 25 Fortune 1000 companies have women CEOs or presidents. Need I go on?

With the new awareness around gender, and women's voices that have sprung from the sexual harassment allegations in Hollywood and beyond, I am hopeful we can create a new reality. A new truth. And, like I said earlier, it seems to me that it's a pivotal time for humanity. The world is ready for a new reality around all things feminine and what it means to be a woman in the 21st century.

Role Play

In some ways, my company is an example of how hard it is to figure all this out. Every day I walk the tightrope of being married, having kids and working, so I get all of those things. I live and breathe it as my own personal reality. One of my greatest hopes is that I can help women discover their power and inspire them to believe they are enough. I want to serve as an example to other women that *I get it, I've been there, I hear you*. My mom always used to say, "To feel loved is to feel understood," and I think this has stayed with me as I attempt to mentor women through the complexities of their lives.

As you can imagine, most of my team members are women and many of them are in that phase of life where they are attempting to be everything to everyone all the time: mother, employee, wife, friend, daughter, etc. And it's difficult to not feel like you are failing at all of it. Anna Quindlen, my pretend great aunt who so often says exactly what I need to hear, wrote in her memoir, *Lots of Candles, Plenty of Cake*, "While the women of our mother's generation felt constrained not to complain that no-wax floors and bridge parties were not exactly stimulating, we didn't want to admit that trying to balance a couple of challenging full-time jobs was kind of a stretch. We were a little happy and a little crazy and a little sad and a little confused." I know these misgivings are not new revelations to be heard.

Many women—just like me and my team members—are managing through the myriad of choices that being a woman born in the 20th century most definitely brings. I was and continue to be well aware of my fortunate circumstances, but until you are in it, doing it, creating it, all the "knowing" in the world can't save you. I am fully aware that I am riding the waves of the previous generations who so valiantly set me and my female peers up for all of these incredible choices. *Thank you, ladies.* Yet all these wonderful choices create a timpani of anxiety that vibrates just under the surface of our beings, creating a pervasive, dull uncertainty that so often brings sadness, insecurity and frustration.

Needless to say, as the founder and leader of my company, it can be hard to find a way to give the women who work with me the flexibility they need. It's something I work at every day. The reality is I do own a business, and businesses need to make money. Here's the tricky part: Balancing the needs of the greater good and the individual can be extremely challenging. I'm constantly asking myself, *How can I be a decisive, responsible, courageous leader who needs to do what is best for the greater good of the company while remaining compassionate and empathetic to the individual?* This is the ultimate paradox and I am not sure I have the answer. But I can say I try. I try as best I can.

So, I meet with my team members as individuals and set up what works for them. And we are honest: It might mean one person doesn't have the same hours as another. With women that's the only way to make it work.

Raising Cinderellas and Cinderfellas

We all have programming. And to be a mother to girls, especially, you have to have an awareness of yourself and your own programming. As if that wasn't challenging enough, you also have external factors that push and pull you along the way. You have to challenge yourself to look at what you might be projecting onto another soul.

It helps to remember, no matter what your story is, your child is not you.

I see so many parents decide their kid is going to be a manifestation of their ego, do what they never could do, complete them somehow. Like, *I was a dancer but never went all the way, so my daughter will.* Your kid is never going to do that. You have to be courageous enough to look inside yourself and ask the question, *How do I help my child become their own self? And am I trying to make them into me?*

A good example is my daughter, Marlie. She has special needs and I have worked hard to come to a sense of peace of accepting her exactly where she is today. Marlie is unique. I've had to struggle with her not conforming to what society preaches as "normal" or "accepted." Many of the topics we have discussed in this chapter have been a battle for her. She struggles with her weight due to taking anti-seizure medication and she doesn't act like the typical 13-year-old girl.

For instance, she has loved cars since she was two years old, and for Halloween she chose to dress up like a race car driver. For a split second I thought about questioning her choice, but caught myself and realized this is not Marlie trying to be a boy—this is Marlie expressing her masculine side and having FUN with it. If there is one thing Marlie has taught me, it's acceptance. She has shown me what living in the present looks like and about finding joy in the simple things. When I see her face light up over the latest Shopkins release, Justin Bieber song or new episode from Dude Perfect, I realize how much joy, spontaneity and fun she has brought me and our family. In some ways, I wish I were more like Marlie. Her first inclination is to always be herself, but later she comes to the realization that it might not be what others expect, whereas for most people it's the other way around. We do what's expected first, act out of expectation first—which creates added anxiety—instead of choosing to live an authentic life.

I know with Marlie I can't push her into something I think she "needs" to be. We seem to be resistant to who our children are—"I wish they were neater, thinner, a better athlete, more talkative." We unknowingly project that onto our kids. They feel it. Their journey is not your journey. If more of us accepted that, we would have more harmony, acceptance and compassion. I challenge you to think about this statement: *What if the exact things that make us different are exactly what we are supposed to bring into this world?* We all have differences. We each have our own individual blueprint that makes us exactly who we are. Sometimes our differences are what make us unique and should be celebrated. Girls especially want to fall in line, but seeing what they like and tuning into their interests is a huge clue to what their purpose in life might be. A lot of times the "imperfections" we see in our children are actually imperfections in ourselves, things we are trying to rectify or relive. I've found that accepting my child exactly as she is—and realizing she is who she was always supposed to be and serving her intended purpose in the universe—has allowed me to let go of all the shoulda, coulda, wouldas that pervade my mind. They say comparison is the thief of joy, so if you remove comparison from your life and your mind, it will set you and your children free.

My 18-year-old son, Harrison, appears to be "all boy" from the outside, yet making assumptions is dangerous because many would be shocked to know he has a strong and well-developed feminine side. He is a writer. And his favorite genre of writing is poetry.

Let a mom brag for a minute.

He is actually quite good at it and has been recognized in his school and our community for some of his work. Harry started writing in middle school and I think he realized it gave him a beautiful outlet to express himself—especially in those fragile adolescent years. I distinctly remember when his friends started to take note of his newfound hobby and nicknamed him "Shakespeare." I talked to him at the time about the new nickname to see if he was OK with it. I guess I was being a paranoid mom and didn't want him to feel "different" (there goes that word again). He told me he was fine with it, but that he was the only boy in his entire school who liked to write. I'm pretty sure it was the first time he realized his expected gender role was not lining up to his reality. I remember giving him my 15-minute sermon on identity, gender and being different; he just looked at me and said, "I know, Mom, chill. I'm not going to stop writing just because not many boys my age write. I'm comfortable being unique." God bless him. What a relief!

Real Life Is Better

All this said, wouldn't it be great, when you hit rock bottom, to have your own personal fairy godmother show up with her magic wand and give you the chance to make all of your dreams come true in an instant? A new man, a new dress, a ride to the party (sounds like my high school fantasy, except we'd be riding to homecoming and having our after-party at Whataburger), just like Cinderella? We women are so happy to believe these myths—that if we can just be more like Cinderella, we'll get everything we want and need. Haven't most of us wished that unicorns were real and life could be beautiful and simple?

In the clarity of full adulthood, we recognize that real life is not only more challenging, but also much more a series of setbacks. In turn, these challenges and the process of learning from them can inspire personal growth and acceptance in our lives.

In my case, a pretty idyllic childhood set me up to expect ease and accomplishment in my endeavors. But before long I was struggling with the expectations: to be a perfect wife, mom, daughter, sister and friend, and to balance my work and personal life seamlessly. I was good at some things, but never perfect.

I also realized life isn't really under my, or anyone's, control. I've learned to expect the unexpected by experiencing some of life's curveballs. My second child has special needs, my mom was diagnosed with breast cancer when I was 18 and has had two recurrences in the past six years, and most recently, I've been struggling with the unexpected death of a close family member. I also came to the realization that my business is much more difficult than I expected it to be. But with every challenge, I've uncovered hidden strengths and I've never felt more enlightened and powerful as a woman who doesn't need to seek out that glass slipper.

Besides, even if I did find it, it would have to be a size 9, so there goes that fairy tale.

ASK YOURSELF

Use these prompts to explore how much you have been duped by the Cinderella myth, how it might have blocked you and how you can eliminate that obstacle to happiness and fulfillment in your life.

1. **Go back.** See if you can remember the first time you questioned your power as a female. Think about a pattern that you started accepting, even though something didn't feel quite right. Did you always have a boyfriend? Some girls are 100 percent convinced they need to have a boyfriend, and they do whatever it takes, including ignoring their feelings. Have you pretended to be unable to do things you actually can do, like drill a hole or solve a problem, because you want to appear helpless and in need of saving? Start changing that thought and behavior, and see if it helps you feel strong and capable.
2. **Look at your guys.** Explore your relationships with the males in your life. Who were you when you interacted with male energy? Did you ever notice that your identity would fall away? Did it trigger

defensiveness or were you true to who you were? I have girlfriends who act completely different around their husbands. When you think about it, I am a walking contradiction. I have this fashion business steeped in femininity and glamour, and I cuss like a trucker. I love pink, but there is so much more than that. This is not all about the external. That's what makes it interesting.

3. **Think about your favorite movies.** Or remember the books you loved growing up. Why did you love them? Did you fantasize that you might be rescued just like so many of the heroines in our culture? Hollywood is actually doing a better job now. *Frozen* is one of the biggest movies Disney has ever made. It debunks the myth that a man is the only way out of danger and into true love. What is important is her love for her sister. And in *Arrival* the love story is quite secondary; the real story is that even with all the pain she knows is in her future, she will choose to live life the way she does. Even *La La Land* broke that Prince Charming mold.

* * *

Chapter 3

MYTH: OTHER WOMEN MUST BE YOUR RIVALS

It's OK to Be Competitive, Have Friends and Still Be a Winner

Women are very complex creatures. And nowhere does that complexity come into play more than when we try to figure out how to function as ambitious, competitive beings in a cutthroat world. In situations where we recognize scarcity—whether it's a job at the top, an award or a house—I don't know about you, but I struggle.

This awareness first hit me when I started playing tennis at a highly competitive level. My nurturing, feminine nature got called into question when I'd see these girls who were out to kick my ass at all costs. I became depressed when I started to realize we weren't all going to hang out, play Pac-Man and eat pizza together before our matches. Obviously, we were all pretty competitive and had earned our way to the top of the Texas tournament circuit, but if truth be told, my ranking never got higher than number 22 in the state. I remained in that comfortable, mediocre spot between being truly great and not so great. Of course I wanted to win, but I wanted to make friends even more. I've always been a pleaser and wanted people to like me (still do). And while I never regretted that having the "killer instinct" wasn't the prominent part of my nature, I did realize that it sets up a conflict between who you are and who you might want to be.

I was at that tough age where I was caught between different desires: I wanted to please my dad by being an elite, ruthless tennis player, yet I yearned to develop friendships, be a girl and have fun. I vividly remember one important match where my dad was frustrated with me. He rarely lost his cool, but I was playing someone he knew I could beat and things just weren't going my way. After the match, he gave it to me straight and said, "E, you just don't have the eye of the tiger." (Yes, you guessed it, the movie *Rocky* was a family favorite back then.) I remember feeling defeated, "less than" and in conflict with myself. On one hand, I wanted so desperately to please my dad, but on the other, I just wanted to have friends and be a normal 12-year-old girl. It's an awkward age, too. I was smack dab in the middle of puberty, trying to summon up the will to kick ass and WIN, while hoping my tan was going to even out after the match and praying my Kotex pad didn't fall out during my next serve. (Cue the *Bridesmaids* tennis scene outtakes.)

Not only was I competing on the court, but I was also competing with my head and my heart. Was being the best what I really wanted or was it what I was supposed to want? Well, as the story goes, I remember playing the next match and blowing it because I was determined to go out there and show my dad how tough I was. I got ahead of myself, forced it and played sloppy tennis. I had little control over my game—a multitude of double faults, too many long balls—and it was a complete disaster. Needless to say, our car ride home was silent. And it was then I knew my dreams of becoming the next Chris Evert were dashed, but at least my pad hung in there for me. (How's that for a silver lining?) My dad did say my tennis outfit was much cuter than those of my opponents. I think that's when he began to accept I was more interested in fashion than tennis.

Speaking of Chris Evert, she was my hero growing up, yet behind her all-American smile and graceful tennis game, I knew we were different. I've always been perplexed by elite professional athletes and their ability to turn off their emotions and access a part of themselves that allows them to detach and develop the killer instinct. For some it might come more naturally, and for others it might be learned and developed over time . . . who knows? However, as I got older, Chris seemed further and further away from someone I could relate to or wanted to be. She once said, "To be a tennis champion, you have to be inflexible. You have to be stubborn. You have to be arrogant. You have to be selfish and self-absorbed. Kind of tunnel vision almost." I guess I wasn't willing to become all those things for the sake of tennis accolades.

Fortunately, Lindsay Vonn (another of my current idols) showed a softer side to her competitive edge. Maybe it's the maturity that comes with age, but I was inspired by her humility at the 2018 Winter Olympics when she lost the super-G after a split-second mistake. I loved her reaction as she skied past the finish line: She looked up to the sky and simply said, "I tried." Awww. The joy of being human. Thank you, Lindsay. And Serena Williams was recently quoted in *Vogue* about being best friends with "her fiercest competitor." "Let's just put an end to this myth that women players cannot be friends," Williams said regarding her BFF and rival, tennis champion Caroline Wozniacki. She went on to explain that having to play against her best friend, and her own sister Venus, didn't get in the way of building lasting friendships with both of them. "It's hard and lonely at the top," she said. "That's why it's so fun to have Caroline and my sister, too."

Don't misunderstand me, though; competition can be a very good thing, and can motivate us to do good in the world. But it can also alienate us. We are all connected. And I believe we are all on this earth to help one another. We need to build each other up, and when someone else succeeds, it needs to be our joy to see them grow. Each of us grows at a different rate. So it's important to not let competition dominate our lives.

Let's explore the light and dark sides of female competition and the reasons why we ultimately need one another.

The Perception of Scarcity

We all know the feeling of scarcity. It's the belief that there is an inadequate supply, a dearth of availability. This perception contributes to the age-old rivalry between women. In an article for psychcentral.com, Lynn Margolies, Ph.D., writes that one theory of why women are competitive in indirectly aggressive ways is attributed to evolutionary psychology. From the beginning of time, women have felt the need to protect themselves from physical harm by using passive-aggressive behavior to lower the status of other women, to continue to be prized by the men who are their sources for survival and identity.

There is some time in our lives, when we get past elementary school age, that we become aware as women that we start to vie for position on a primal, cellular, even biological feeling of scarcity. We come to an awareness that there might not be enough to go around, and we also start to feel marginalized, in the minority. It manifests differently for different people, but we start trying to manipulate our friends, our behavior, our beauty. Some girls will ostracize other girls or groups of girls so that they feel more powerful in their group. Seems to me it starts around seventh grade, although some research is showing it can start as early as preschool. And while it's a very female part of growing up and might even be unconscious, it can be painful on both sides.

For my part, I tried to combat this sneaky meanness and overcompensated by always being friendly and funny. I figured I would just *nice* the crap out of them. And one can never underestimate the power of humor. It's my antidote against all things negative. I'm not sure where I would be without it . . . maybe still getting my ass whooped on the tennis court with no friends. But the point is, the Golden Rule of friendship states that if you make people feel good about themselves, they will like you—and laughter does just that. It makes you feel good about yourself and the person who triggered your laughter.

But being "nicey nice" and funny is only effective for so long. Once adulthood hits, pulling the "I am nice" card is like showing a full house to a royal flush. The rules of the game have gotten more complicated; women are more experienced and have more on the line to lose at home and at work. I saw this in college and in my early career. Women start to confront the reality of their future—their relationship prospects and career opportunities—and it gets real, REAL FAST. I've had to learn the hard way, over many years, the value of building boundaries and detaching more. I recognize that I'm a pleaser. But I've also realized I'm not going to be able to fix everything and everyone. And most certainly, not everyone is going to like me no matter how hard I try. They might not even like my vulgar sense of humor (which is really f*ing unfortunate). So I decided along the way that I'm not responsible for other people's behavior. I'm only responsible for my reaction to it. This has freed me from so much anxiety and hardship.

Why Are We So Hungry?

A lot of this competitive behavior might go back to not having good role models. Maybe it's just another way of internalizing the fairy tales we grew up with. Cinderella certainly had to keep her eye on her stepmother and stepsisters, and Snow White had one nasty stepmother herself, who was clearly out to get her. Even though society has progressed, survival of the fittest has been around as long as humanity began; it's only natural to protect yourself and your tribe at all costs.

In my company, which is primarily composed of women, I see a natural tendency for people to split off into little factions, bonded tribes. Give a group of women six months together, and all of a sudden they're going to lunch together, peeing together and menstruating together. It's like an estrogen den. My poor husband is convinced he might start having a period. He spends so much time around women, he's started to keep a box of Kleenex in his office just in case tears come. (He also has a box of tampons just in case he does, in fact, get his period! We all know it's better to be prepared than to force a friend to trail you to the bathroom.)

It's natural for rivalries and competition for attention to emerge, so I've intentionally tried my hardest to create a culture without a perception of scarcity. We all know there is a dearth of women at the top in most male-dominated workplaces, but I've also come to understand that there is this perception that your place or role at work is constantly being threatened by other women who want to grab it. As a leader, I do everything I can to instill the idea that my attention is not limited to only a few, and that there's more room at the top for growth. I've worked hard at cultivating the idea that if you show me that you can be my next vice president, then by God, you will be! If you work for me, you have a voice, and I've come to find over the years that this alone can propel someone way beyond a title or corner office. All it takes is the courage to speak. A woman who started as my intern became my EVP eight years later, so trust me when I say EVERYONE has a voice in my office.

Compare and Despair

If you ask me, still another theory of female competition lies in how we see ourselves. Feelings of lack, insecurity and low confidence tend to hinder those perspectives. For so many of us, we look at other women and see something we wish we could have—thinner legs, a bigger house, a cuter husband, a daughter who doesn't tell the waiter her vagina hurts, or a son who doesn't break every bone in his body on the regular. You name it, and a woman has thought it.

But when we do this, we aren't seeing anyone at all. It does something very dangerous: It dehumanizes the other. Sadly, the only thing we end up seeing is our misguided attempt at feeling "enough." We don't know her story, her truth. We live in a world of perfectly curated, false versions of reality. We see a few moments of someone's day and fill in the rest with fantasy that we like to dress up as "reality." These assumptions we make of others lead us down a slippery slope. The compare-and-contrast game is unwinnable and superfluous and takes us to a place of guilt, insecurity and sadness. How many times have you regretted saying something about someone or assumed you knew the truth, yet when you experienced the person on your own, you realized how misguided you were and that all-encompassing feeling of remorse takes hold? I know I have.

A couple of years ago, I gave a speech to a group of entrepreneurs, and most of them were women. There was part of my speech where I discussed women and our tendencies to compare ourselves to one another. Here's what I said: "I could go on and on about how we females tend to pit one another against each other. I believe it's all fear-based and stems from a deep-seated feeling of lack. We all do it; we assume we have the other person figured out, but in actuality we know nothing about the other person's reality and why they make the decisions they make."

Why does Mary bring all her kids to every school event? Her kids are so rambunctious and disruptive.

Why does Elaine not come to every lacrosse game? She's an absentee mom.

Why does Sue volunteer 24/7 at the school? It's a little odd—does she have a life?

The answers could be:

Mary is a single mother and cannot afford childcare.

Elaine has a special needs daughter and cannot leave her at home alone at 7 p.m. when the games are being played.

Sue's husband travels 24/7 and she needs to sink her heart and soul into a purpose.

See how when you take a step back and realize we are all human beings dealing with what life has dealt us, it allows for more grace and compassion to enter into the conversation? Let's all focus on being the heroes of our own stories rather than invading and creating false narratives around other people's stories.

I have had my own journey around this; we all have. For instance, I occasionally feel house envy. It's just natural to look outside of yourself and think, *Oh, if I had that, I'd be happier*, but who knows what is going on behind the scenes? I have a good friend who was house hunting a couple of years ago and looked at a wonderful house that she absolutely fell in love with, but it was beyond her budget. She told another friend about the house and how much she loved it. Well, that friend ended up buying the house. She could afford it, and it has been a great house for her family, but that was a tough situation because one would inevitably compare and feel "less than."

The outcome really sucked for my friend; we shared lots of wine drinking and biting our tongues to not wish her friend ill. But the reality is, this is life and we have to remain faithful in our own personal journeys. (Truth be told, while we were drinking and crying over the house, we concocted about 20 stories of how awful her life really must be: cheating husband, chronic vaginal dryness . . . you name it, she had it. If you're wondering, in my book this isn't gossiping or demeaning. This is called survival.)

The Appearance of Perfection

Sometimes I look at other female entrepreneurs and feel business envy! Tory Burch, for instance, seems like she has it all going on. She's gorgeous, thin, rich . . . but who knows what's happening behind the shiny gold "T" logo? I assume her company and life are all smooth sailing, but I also know that making assumptions is dangerous.

One of my favorite books is *The Four Agreements* by Don Miguel Ruiz. In the book, he lays out four agreements we must make with ourselves in order to live more peaceful lives. His third agreement is *Don't Make Assumptions.* He states: "The problem with making assumptions is that we believe they are the truth! We invent a whole story that's only truth for us, but we *believe* it. One assumption leads to another assumption; we jump to conclusions, and we take our story very personally." I bring this to mind when I find myself jumping to unproven conclusions about someone else. When I do this, I try to catch myself and realize the only thing I can do is look at my own truth and what works for me and my family. That's it, period, the end.

And a big help for me is all the lessons I've learned around my daughter. I tend to look outside myself and see women with these incredible (or so-called incredible) mother/daughter relationships. Their journey seems so ideal—joining charity groups together, shopping together, going on girls' trips . . . . I don't have that as much with my daughter and it's caused a lot of heartache for me. But I've learned to stop myself before the pain gets too big, and recognize what I do have is perfect. It's perfect for me. God sent her to me and I was sent to her. We were meant to be together on this earth to learn and guide each other through life's uncertain waters and there is where *I find the light*. The one thing I know for sure (OK, cue Oprah) is without her, I wouldn't be the person I am today and I'm pretty sure I wouldn't be writing this book. So, thank you, Marlie, for being my beautiful, one-of-a-kind daughter. I love you.

Mommy Mean Girls

Ugh. The dreaded phrase. We've all encountered Mean Girls and suffered under their indifference, condescending eye rolls or direct hostility, and yet, if we're honest with ourselves, we've all probably wished we would have behaved differently in certain situations around other women. Tina Fey says it best in her movie *Mean Girls*: "You all have got to stop calling each other sluts and whores. It just makes it OK for guys to call you sluts and whores." I love that because it's so true. If we end up pitting each other against each other, we all lose—and even worse, we lose to the boys.

Ambition shouldn't be a dirty word. But if a woman displays so-called aggressive or overly driven traits, she is usually referred to as a "bitch," whereas a man is considered a hard-nosed businessman. Such bullshit. And a massive double standard. It's impossible to win this race. I tend to get so confused as to what a woman is even supposed to be in today's world. From what I can tell, we're supposed to be pretty, nice, skinny, successful (but only in a well-understood, easy-to-digest way), sexy and sexual (but only enough to not offend anyone), productive (be able to do and be it all), and to top it off, supportive of our husband and family. BARF. Can you imagine a man living under these expectations? Most men can't even combat the common cold, much less meet up to these impossible standards. (I had to get a little male bashing in here . . . give me grace.)

To be honest, Mean Girls never really go away, no matter what phase of life we're in. You get through high school thinking it's all over because you don't have to regularly cohabitate with people who saw you in headgear, but alas, the Mommy Mean Girls appear. You know, the ones who have probably never had a mother f*ing Pinterest fail, who practically sideswipe you in the grocery store when they eye gluten, dairy, soy or anything with flavor in your cart. The mommies with perfect children who would never admit to dealing with tantrums or feeding their child a Toaster Strudel (Gretchen Wieners, anyone?) and bean burrito for dinner. Hello, MOTHERHOOD IS EXHAUSTING and frozen things are easy. It's hard to swallow, but it's a reality many of us face. We tend to fall into using our children as another way to establish dominance and compete with other women, whether it's about our kids learning to roll over, reading kindergarten sight words, or receiving college acceptance letters.

Just as I've had to navigate a world of Mommy Mean Girls, I've also had to find a way to navigate competition in the workplace and believe me, I've experienced some toxic situations. Early in my career, in Dallas, I was working under a female boss, and I really had to make an effort to get her to accept me. I was her assistant and there was a power struggle about how much she was willing to relegate to me, and it was a very uncomfortable situation. She was insecure; so was I. She was at the height of her career, wanting to build financial security, and I was at the start. It was almost a cliché, because her husband ended up hitting on me and I had to tell the CEO of the company that he was harassing me. My boss and her husband ended up divorcing and she lost her job. This experience scarred me and I ended up leaving that company and heading to New York. Sadly, I had more learning to do in the Big Apple . . . .

In New York, I worked for a woman whom I saw as the ultimate designer. She was artsy, cool, intellectual and an extremely talented artist. However, and much to my dismay, I soon began to see that she quickly labeled me as shallow and definitely not as smart as she was. She saw me as the quintessential Texas girl—cute, perky and most likely a little light upstairs. Even though I looked up to her and I felt I could have done great work for her, she never gave me a chance. I was miserable but trying hard to hang on. One day, after I arrived five minutes late to work, she pulled me aside and screamed at me for my unprofessionalism.

Well, that was it. I cracked. I broke. I literally had never cried at work up to that point. The flood gates opened up. I was a goner. I cried that real ugly cry where you realize you can't breathe and you get splotchy all over. I was mortified. I could tell she was stunned, shocked and possibly a little pleased. She got me.

Soon after that incident, I began looking for another job and found one; ironically I worked for a man I adored and ended up staying in that job for more than four years. The moral of the story is *shit happens* and it takes these experiences to make you stronger, wiser and—believe it or not—more confident.

All of this has inspired me to do what I can in my corner of the world to shine the light on another way of being. For instance, at Elaine Turner, I preach toward a transparent culture, one defined by open communication, accountability and honesty. I show my staff that I am accessible and compassionate and that I will listen to direct, open communication, even if it's uncomfortable, and with luck we can move forward with an understanding. My hope is this will alleviate a lot of the fear.

The one thing I ask of my staff is that they never be unprofessional or unkind. In my eyes, it's never worth being cruel, ever. I walk into difficult conversations with a genuine interest in hearing the other side and being accountable for my part in any frustration that potentially pops up. However, I also expect the same in return—most things in life are not one-way streets, even at work. We are all engaging in two-way relationships that ebb and flow. Rarely are we mind readers, so effective communication is essential in creating a work environment that prospers.

A certain amount of healthy competition is human. People have always competed—for survival, for position, for status. Where I draw the line is not ambition. It's when I sense something toxic going on under the surface. I'm much better with someone who is honest, open and kind saying, "I love this company and I want to work my way up"—I'm always "YES!" But if you try to manipulate, it's not going to work. For me, it's best for my staff to be open about how they want to grow their careers rather than create an under-the-radar power play.

You're OUT

Occasionally, I do see negative energy infiltrate my business, and I have come to the conclusion over time that it's best to nip it in the bud immediately. I used to wait too long and give people the benefit of the doubt. I would say things to myself like *Well, they just had a bad day* or *That's not their typical behavior*, but now I cut if off at the start. It's classic passive-aggressive behavior and it can build like a funnel cloud. If I see it, I find it's best to head it off because one person's energy—negative or positive—can change a culture. Sometimes after a long time of trying, it just doesn't work, and that person doesn't stay at Elaine Turner.

I've learned the hard way that I have to lay the ground rules early on—what works and what doesn't work. I make no qualms about being in a unique position where I have the power to do just that. There are many amazing women out there who have to live and work under conditions that they have zero control over creating or managing. This is a challenge, and one for which I have deep empathy.

I decided early on that I wanted to support those women. I want my overall philosophy about interacting with my office staff to extend in some regard to my customer. We've always trained our salespeople to be kind, understanding and respectful. Nothing is worse than a salesperson looking down their nose at or ignoring a potential customer. I feel strongly that our clients have taken the time to step into my store, and by God, they will be honored, whether they purchase anything or not.

We always talk about our customer and how we can support them in their lifestyle. Recently, we began to see that many women no longer have time to browse through brick-and-mortar retail stores. In most cases, they are turning to the Internet to shop. We realized that it was quick and convenient for them, but we also thought perhaps it was a little impersonal and that a customer might miss the interaction with someone interested in helping her select and acquire items she may want.

We had many in-depth meetings about creating a concierge-type sales model that would satisfy the preferences of each individual shopper. We call this Elaine Turner Elite, and we have hired stylists across the country to help us implement this new way of shopping. Some women would like to have a stylist come to their home or office for a personal consultation. Other women would rather the stylist send them a customized collection of items that they can try or pick through whenever they have time. Others may want the stylist to advise them about how they might purchase an item from the website. In any regard, it's another opportunity for me to help and empower women who come across my path and touch my life.

What the Experts Say

Experts say that two things could be going on in work/life situations that feel toxic:

1. Bullying behavior from your female boss (or friend) might be psychological—e.g., she doesn't believe in her own capabilities and so views you and your talents and accomplishments as a threat, so she must put you down all the time. (And note that this might be affecting how you deal with your female staff, if you are a manager.)
2. There is a scarcity of women at the top in most male-dominated workplaces, yes, but there is also the perception that your place is constantly being threatened by other women who want to grab it.

Executive coach Bonnie Marcus writes in *Forbes*[1] that "If we lack the confidence in our innate talent to help us reach our goals, we are more competitive and anyone is a potential threat, especially other women in a workplace that fails to offer sufficient advancement opportunity . . . But if you think about it, almost every working woman in America read fairy tales like Snow White or Cinderella. So it's not like we haven't seen women trying to banish other women for their beauty and hopefully their talent.

[1]forbes.com/sites/bonniemarcus/2016/01/13/the-dark-side-of-female-rivalry-in-the-workplace-and-what-to-do-about-it/#3ae527b15255

But the idea of destroying our competition goes very deep within our psyche and the messaging of our culture. We pretend we don't do it. Because when you're raised to be a good girl, you wouldn't do anything that nasty or unsettling."

And while most will agree that men are very competitive, they tend to be more overtly competitive. Katherine Crowley and Kathi Elster, co-authors of *Mean Girls at Work: How to Stay Professional When Things Get Personal*, state that "women are complicated. While most of us want to be kind and nurturing, we struggle with our darker side, feelings of jealousy, envy and competition. While men tend to compete in an overt manner—jockeying for position and fight[ing] to be crowned 'winners'— women often compete more covertly and behind the scenes. This covert competition and indirect aggression is at the heart of mean behavior among women at work."

Susan Shapiro Barash states: "We need to finally admit there's a problem. To finally say, Hello, can everyone admit that whether it's your friend telling you she's engaged or pregnant or her kid got into Harvard or whatever she tells you that seems so incredibly close to a goal of yours that you haven't achieved, to stop secretly seething? Take a look at your own life and say, 'Well, she's achieved this. What do I need to do? Not because she has it, but because I need this.' And it doesn't have to be the same thing at all. We need to stop contrasting and comparing."

There is also this freedom we can allow ourselves to experience when we hop off the hamster wheel of comparing. The truth is someone will ALWAYS have something you want—I mean, shit, I'm still waiting for my perky boobs and my renovated kitchen to appear—but the things I have right now are things someone else is currently dreaming of. We have to find resolve within ourselves to admire from afar, but be most connected to and OK with where we are and what we have achieved right now. All the accolades, honor-student bumper stickers, promotions and "stuff" didn't just appear; they were all earned—unless you were a trust fund baby... and in that case, have I mentioned my perky boobs and kitchen reno? Joking. It is one of life's hardest lessons, but we have to find space in our hearts to find genuine joy for other's successes because there truly is room at the top for everyone, and our time will come.

The Truth Is...

We need each other. I know I've talked a lot about how and why women struggle with one another in this chapter, but the truth is we wouldn't be whole without each other's support, friendship, mentorship and sisterhood. "Dreams change, trends come and go," muses *Sex and the City's* Carrie Bradshaw, "but friendships never go out of style." I don't know where I would be without my girlfriends and our wine nights—the emotional cleansing that usually takes place with little or no resistance; earthy discussions surrounding all things vaginas, uteruses and hormones; tips and advice on the latest juice cleanse, anti-aging serum and hair removal procedure. This is what gets me to tomorrow.

We all know that our friendships with the most important women in our lives are often our deepest and most profound love stories. I love the way Shauna Niequist (author and speaker) describes friendship as "carrying the mess together." All of it—the secrets, hardships, darkness and regrets. As friends, we gladly take on each other's pain so we no longer have to hide or feel ashamed. When we fully and completely embrace the sanctity of friendship, we invite the light of unconditional love and acceptance to shine right through our brokenness. We are stripped down, exposed and open to its miraculous healing and grace. This is what true friendship feels like for me.

As women, we get it. We all have an unspoken understanding of what it means to be a woman: the overwhelming impossibility of it all; our sensitive, vulnerable, breakable hearts; our complicated body and lady parts; our innate drive for perfectionism; our desire to be the best damn mother in the world and the unbound, infinite love we have for our children; and our dutiful, caretaking spirit. I guess you could say intimacy begets intimacy, and a newfound emphasis on female support and friendship isn't just good for some women—it's good for all women.

With this new awareness around bringing more women into boardrooms, government and Hollywood leading roles, I am hopeful we are on our way to real, tangible change. If we create an arguably stronger cultural focus around women, I believe female friendships, mentorships and overall support for one another can multiply. As a result, helping women increase their professional power and fulfill their higher potential could create a ripple affect that subsequently reduces gender inequality. When women work together, they also succeed together. We all NEED to embrace the Tina Fey/ Amy Poehler, Gayle/Oprah love fests! Celebrating female friendship, rather than competition between women, will help the next generation of women embrace, rather than resent, the strong women around them.

This calls for a wine night. Who's in?!

ASK YOURSELF

Relationships with other women can be difficult if you feel you are always competing. Let's take a look at some questions you can explore:

1. **Have you ever had a female boss?** Or have you been one? What was that experience like? Did you notice any differences between how you dealt with situations with her compared with a male boss? And if you are a boss, do you notice your female staff treating you differently from how they treat a male?
2. **Do you feel competitive with your friends** about your kids' accomplishments, your vacation plans, your home? Can you detach emotionally and acknowledge that she has some things you

might want, and if you need them, too, what it would take? Not to push her off her throne, but to get what you want, openly?

3. The flip side—the light side, if you will—is that our female relationships become a huge part of our support system. We invest in each other. And as a result, women tend to live longer, because social connection is so healthy and necessary for a healthy life. **What are the relationships you have cultivated, and how can you nourish them so they stay healthy?**
4. Let's flip things around a bit again. **Has there ever been a time in your life when you glossed over the truth in an effort to protect yourself?** Did you have an opportunity to share a struggle but instead chose to fib a little to make it seem like you had it all together? It can be so liberating to open up about your weaknesses and failures, both for you and the people you are connecting with. How many times have you felt alone in your feat? How much more empowered and supported would you have felt if someone had said, "Girl, I've been there, too" or "My vacation pictures look like magic, but the truth is we all hated each other two days in." Fantasy-painted pictures add fuel to the competitive fire. Be honest about your reality and slow the burn.

* * *

Chapter 4

MYTH: VULNERABILITY = WEAKNESS

Living With Too Much of the "Feels"

The quote "It's both a blessing and a curse to feel everything so deeply" has always resonated with me. I've constantly wondered why I feel a little more than most people and why I process more through my heart than my head. I am somewhat of a paradox in that I love people and connection, but I always have my guard up, always finding myself in protection mode. I've continually felt a little exposed, a little fragile, a little afraid. For whatever reason, I know I can sense and feel pain, darkness and negative emotions more than most people. It's hard to describe and it's exhausting. But I've come to understand it's me.

In the field of modern psychology, some might say I am a "highly sensitive person" (HSP, for short) or even an "empath." But whatever it is, it's overwhelming. Sometimes I know why I feel things so deeply and sometimes I don't. To complicate matters even more, somehow a part of me knows how others are feeling, too. And here's the hard part: A lot of the time I can't distinguish between my own emotions and the emotions of others. The more those lines become blurred, the more confused I become and my confidence and sense of self begin to suffer.

Laughin' on the Outside

Ironically, when people meet me, they tend to see me as an extrovert. They automatically think, *She's a fashion designer, gives public speeches and hosts events at her stores—she must be an extrovert.* But that's only a half-truth. Yes, I do love people; I love making people laugh and sharing my creativity with others. The reality is, though, I actively seek solitude and enjoy being alone. I push hard for periods of time and then I rest for periods of time. This is why I don't work out as much as I should—my life is already a StairMaster.

The positive aspects of my journey as an empath have come with age. Now that I'm older and know myself better, I have started to perceive my intense sensitivity as my own personal superpower. Having a stronger tendency toward empathy has given me a leg up on the emotional intelligence scale, or as we now refer to it, a high EQ. I can remember my mom talking to me about emotional intelligence before it became a "thing." This was in the mid-1970s and not much was being talked about yet with regard to emotional IQ. But my mom knew about the research and would gladly preach to me and my siblings about my high EQ. Looking back, I never quite knew what the hell she was talking about, but I took the compliment anyway. I guess my easy access to tears and occasional emotional outbursts led her to believe I had a gift rather than a lack of emotional regulation.

As hard as it was to feel so damn much, I'm very lucky. I have a set of incredibly evolved and progressive parents. They did their best to validate my depth of emotion, even if my mom did love to tell me how "sensitive" I was when movies pulled at my heartstrings a little too intensely. The old adage that most of the people who play a significant role in our lives are here to teach or help us in some way really rings true when I think about the role my mom has played in my life, and the kind of mother she prepared me to be by embracing my empathic nature and allowing me the chance to experience vulnerability.

After years of learning about my emotional stability —*being emotional does NOT make you unstable, my friends*—I have come to a place of acceptance and understanding of why I'm built the way I am. I now can see how all the pieces have lined up before me. It's as if my life up until Marlie's birth was preparing me to be her mother all along. All those years, all that deep emotion, all that confusion, I see now, was my own personal divine "setup." I guess I did need my extreme sensitivity all along. It has allowed me to unlock my higher self and access the deepest reservoirs of empathy and compassion that I have within me, and I humbly believe this to be my most significant offering to the world and to people around me.

Cartwheeling Into Vulnerability

Like all of us, I too have had my own painful experiences with vulnerability. For whatever reason these pivotal, transformational moments leave permanent, indelible marks on our soul. One of these moments happened to me at age 15. I knew that making the high school varsity cheerleading squad would be difficult, so I started practicing in my sophomore year. I attended a large public high school in a small suburb located outside of Houston, Texas. Picture *Friday Night Lights*, the television series that followed a high school football team in the small town of Odessa, Texas. That was pretty much my reality.

As most people know, Texas and cheerleading go hand in hand, and being a cheerleader is rather in line with running for mayor, dating the quarterback of the football team or winning the lottery. It's big, like the-size-of-the-state kind of big. It brought with it a certain amount of cachet; if you were a cheerleader, you automatically held a position of rank in your high school and community.

To say the least, I was stressed.

In our school, we had around 2,500 students and we competed at the highest level of sports competition in the state. I went to high school in the late '80s and it was around that time that cheerleading began to change from simply being a popularity contest to a highly respected sport for well-tuned athletes and skilled gymnasts.

Needless to say, our varsity cheer squad was really good. They won awards, traveled and had nationally renowned gymnasts and athletes on the team. The good news was that I had already made the junior varsity team my sophomore year, but making varsity was taking it to another level. Depending on the spots available and how many seniors were graduating, it could be hard to secure a spot. To make matters worse, our cheerleading squad was selected by the entire student body.

Yes, you heard me: The entire student body watched and chose who would be a cheerleader. Have you ever felt like your stomach just squeezed itself into the size of a marble? Be 15, with braces, a perm and a little spunk, then stand in front of 2,500 judgmental teenagers and let them decide your fate. To say I was feeling vulnerable (and a little sick to my stomach) is an understatement.

As far as my skills were concerned, I was average. My strengths included my loud voice, physical strength, highly coiffed perm and peppy spirit. My weaknesses were my sub-par gymnastics skills and resounding lack of flexibility, which often resulted in below-average jumps and rigid moves. You see, I had spent much of my life on the tennis court and in the pool, both of which required very different skill sets.

Now that I've set the stage, I think you can imagine what's coming. After training for months, I never could muster up the courage to do a back flip (nope, not even one). And this after my parents paid for weeks of tumbling lessons. You see, I had (and still have) this very realistic fear of breaking my f*ing neck. It is not natural to blindly flip backwards in the air and land on your feet. I'm not a cat person, I'm a dog person. Dog people don't do flips. We prance, we pose, we bark loudly and we seek affection. No matter how hard I ran or how tightly I clenched my jaw, something always stopped me from hurtling myself into the air. This challenge seemed insurmountable, and suddenly the varsity cheer squad seemed like a tree I shouldn't be barking up.

I slowly began to psych myself out and became more and more discouraged. I even began to anticipate the moment of rejection. I could almost feel it . . . and it hadn't even happened yet. Looking back now, I think it was the first time in my life I wasn't able to conquer my physical skills and achieve what I set my mind to. I think much of it had to do with my age. Being smack-dab in the middle of my early teen years, the ignorance of childhood had started to fade and the realities of becoming an adult were setting in. At this age, you have experienced enough to know and understand the reality of rejection, being judged and feeling shame. When you're a small child, you just hold your nose, jump into the deep end and hope for the best, but life and time squash that ignorant yet blissful stage. Fear starts to become a very acute reality in a very new way. Fear transforms from monsters under your bed or not getting to ride the bus next to your best friend into fear of failure, fear of things out of your control and, again, fear of breaking your neck.

Riddled with anxiety and tamed with hairspray, I arrived at tryout day. As I walked into the gym, I immediately saw several of the girls doing powerful roundoffs followed by consecutive flip-flops; you could hardly see their bodies they were moving so fast. My heart sank. I thought to myself, *What the hell am I doing here?* I swear to this day I thought I was going up against Mary Lou Retton, but I'm almost sure she didn't attend my high school. I immediately thought, *I am a complete fraud*, and for a split second I had an "I, Tonya" moment and thought about looking for a baton to take out the competition.

The reality was, over the past couple of months of practicing, I had allowed myself to go down a dark path of insecurity. I just didn't feel I was good enough, and if truth be told, on that day I wasn't. When my turn came up, I froze, and for a second I actually thought about walking away. But I went ahead and accepted my fate. By the time I finished my lame, single roundoff entrance (basically a cartwheel), I was so winded I could barely breathe. No words were coming out of my mouth. I barely got through my routine, but once I did, I ran to the bathroom and cried. I knew I had failed. And I was right; at 3:15 that afternoon, my name was never called. I was the only sophomore girl on JV to not make the varsity squad. I remember feeling shame, embarrassment and grief, and hardest-hitting of all, failure. I went home and didn't come out of my room for days.

Here's the lesson in all of this. It was my first EPIC fail. And oh-so luckily for me, it was in front of the entire student body. But guess what? I survived and I learned a lot about myself. I learned I could recover. I learned I could survive failure. I learned I could survive rejection. I learned I could SURVIVE, period. As Tina Fey says, "You've got to experience failure to understand you can survive it." Well, I survived it in an old musty gym in Sugarland, Texas, at the young age of 15. Sure, my confidence was a little beaten up, but my hair was practically unscathed (silver lining courtesy of Breck hairspray).

Back from Pity City

After a week of feeling sorry for myself, I picked myself up and tried out for the drill team. One of my good friends and mentors always says, "You can visit Pity City, but you can't live there." So I chose to move. I moved to a place of some much needed "shame resilience," as sociologist and author Brené Brown would say. I recognized that even though I was hurt and disappointed and maybe even downright devastated, my success and recognition were not tied to the approval of others. My value was based on courage. And I was just wildly courageous. Bye-bye shame. You aren't needed here anymore.

To make a long story short, I ended up making the drill team and had an incredible year. I met a lot of new people and learned to dance a little better, too. As the story goes, time heals and the pain got more manageable. I built my confidence back up over the school year and decided to try out for varsity cheerleader again.

I know, you're probably thinking, *Why would she do this to herself again?* But the old adage is true: *You'd better get back on the horse that bucked you or risk never being in the arena again.* By the time tryouts arrived that April, I remember feeling like I had nothing to lose. I'd been through the worst of it, and even then my stomach seemed to return to its normal size. So why not go for it again?

All went much better. I came out with confidence, I owned my tumbling deficiency and compensated with my loud, cheerful voice and perfected perm and won them over. I got my wish of being a senior varsity cheerleader and the rest is history. But more than anything else, I got myself back. That part of myself that knew "I was enough" regardless of what 2,500 teenagers thought the year before.

Gender Fluidity: Marriage, Parenthood and the Transformation of Male/Female Roles

Throughout our lives there is an ebb and flow to vulnerability. As our roles shift, a new load of vulnerability comes with it. It seems as though once you conquer one challenge, you are presented with another. After my braces were plucked off, my perm flattened out and my cheerleading days ended, I jumped into another role of vulnerability: wife.

After the honeymoon was over and the joy of unboxing Pyrex waned, a new life started. This new life started to feel like a vulnerability bomb. Beyond the "Should I pee with the door open or closed?" you start to wade in unchartered waters of what roles you play in your marriage. Sure, society has given you lots of fantasized versions, but what is the right fit for you? What will make your marriage sustainable and keep you true to yourself? This marriage shit is not easy, even from the start.

My husband, Jim, is a good ol' Midwestern boy brought up on a good work ethic and whole-fat milk. He likes numbers and order, but he has a big heart and isn't afraid to feel feelings. And me, I shoulda, coulda, woulda been Miss Texas: big hair, big personality and also not afraid to feel feelings. We found our groove pretty quickly—who takes out the trash, balances the checkbook, cooks, cleans. Hell, once we even figured out the whole "open or closed restroom door" thing, we thought we had all of life's answers. So much so that we started a business and then did something even crazier . . . we had kids.

If marriage is a vulnerability bomb, then parenthood is nuclear. Never have I experienced more moments of vulnerability, and sometimes that vulnerability leads to even more vulnerability. (WTF?!) We found ourselves questioning so much of what we believed about roles of men and women in parenthood, and men and women in general. To be honest, I'm not even sure I was aware of it at the time, because when that nuclear baby hits your house, it is survival mode 24/7. There were some very clear moments where we felt society pushed us one way, while our vulnerable hearts and predisposition pulled us the other way.

As we all know, there seems to be this mythology in our society—to me it's almost a puritanical, Western way of thinking—that vulnerability is not acceptable. That to be successful, you have to be tough and convince everyone around you that you have it all together. Both men and women are in on this "fake it till you make it" game, but the male/female dynamics and society's misguided norms are severely limiting the roles we are "allowed" to play. These limited roles make us feel like failures when we don't measure up or feel fulfilled by what society has told us we should want or do.

Taking it back to those early days, these society-defined guidelines of my role as a mother and wife almost killed my husband. No, really, he almost died. After my being cooped up in a house with a GIANT screaming baby, not being able to sit without an inflatable donut (did I mention my baby was giant?), and never acknowledging the difference between day and night, I hit a wall. Well, technically, my breast pump hit a wall. I had a meltdown and threw my f*ing pump down the stairs. Jim was spared by mere inches. Can you imagine that headline?

"DESIGNER KILLS HUSBAND WITH BREAST PUMP." Sore nipples everywhere would have rejoiced because they finally read news that felt relevant. News that let them know it was OK to hate pumping, to feel tired and lost. To feel VULNERABLE.

But thank God there was no death by breast pump, because without Jim I couldn't have survived motherhood. He faced his own vulnerabilities and we experienced newness together. He actually took on a lot of things society places in the mother's hands. He did, and still does, a lot of things that may not be the norm for most men. He works with me (and a shitload of other women). He slept with our infant daughter, Marlie, for six months and bottlefed her (formula, because the pump was broken, ha ha). He also buys my monthly supply of tampons and his "shop talk" is about bags and shoes. He conformed to what our family needed instead of what society told him we needed. It takes balls to be that vulnerable.

Tough Guys Don't Always Win

But why? Why does it take *balls* to do things society says you don't need balls to do? Throughout modern history our heroes have been men like Clint Eastwood and Al Pacino, or at least played by them. In the folklore Wild West of Wild Bill Hickok and Jesse James, any cracks could get you killed; Tony Soprano's tough-guy exterior belied the anxiety that seethed within him and that only his therapist really knew about.

But guess what? These guys were mostly outlaws, and to my mind, all fairy tales, not examples of how to live an authentic, full life. They don't seem like men I'd like to be, emulate or even really know. The good news is, I see and even feel it starting to change. This so-called "toughness" and strict adherence to past ideas and expectations around what it means to be a man seem to be much less cherished now than they used to be.

Being from Texas has exposed me to a certain type of machismo mentality; there's a lot of hunting, fishing, guns and big trucks in our great state. Honestly, though, I love Texas, and sorry guys, but it really is *like a whole other country*. We even have our own language, y'all. Texas has taught me to hold my own and find my power in a historically male-dominated culture. Ironically, even though the reality of these stereotypes can be challenging, you also discover another side to what's really going on when you go deeper. Texas men are strong and independent-minded. Yet from where I sit, I can see they like their women strong, too. Anne Richards was no slouch, and just look at Chip and Joanna Gaines on HGTV's *Fixer Upper*—she's all in on "demo day" and can hold a hammer like no woman I've ever seen.

Thankfully, I've had a good 47 years on this planet living my very own social science experiment, like the rest of you. I have experienced firsthand what it feels like to exist in a world with less-defined roles for both men and women. The 21st century has brought a sense of liberation surrounding the roles we play in all facets of our lives: marriage, work and child rearing.

Yet as much as we feel released by the outdated, oversimplified male/female roles placed on our parents' generation, we are also left with the collateral damage of trying to figure out what to do with all these choices. Inevitably, uncertainty, murkiness and ambiguity run amok, which usually leads to an increase in our therapy bills, Prozac dosage and wine intake. I realize change can bring fear, and fear can create unpredictable behavior, anxiety and discontent. Simply existing in today's environment can feel heavy, chaotic and scary. Sometimes it feels like the world is at a standstill of uncertainty, and global division feels polarizing.

But through all of this negative perception, I still believe. I believe in the inevitable expansion of the universe and human consciousness. Therefore, when things appear to be in a state of retraction or moving in reverse, the world is still moving forward. We are here to learn, grow and evolve (at least that's what I am choosing to believe), and these so-called moments of regression are simply part of the larger, universal narrative taking place that is here to teach us and propel us into the future, not the past.

And it takes some patience, too. I like to think that life is a long term, step-by-step gig; change, growth and improvement tend to happen incrementally. One thing that sets so many of us up for disappointment and unhappiness is living in a world where we believe positive change should happen overnight. We live in a NOW culture. I just started a new job; where's my raise? My husband graduated law school; what house should we buy? I started my child in speech therapy; now he can get ahead of his peers. I gained five pounds over the holidays; I'll lose it this week. It goes on and on. Life doesn't work that way. We have to force ourselves to stop and see the small steps.

Baby Steps Toward Opening Up

My daughter, Marlie, has been my greatest teacher in showing me how seemingly insignificant, everyday gains are vital in building a healthy perspective. Every single day I watch her conquer and achieve small tasks, and these small wins result in big wins. This small change in perception has altered the course of my life and how I operate within it. It's the same in the male/female vulnerability game. We have spent a lifetime building up a defensive armor of toughness, especially as women operating in a male-dominated society. But then again, men are vulnerable, too. They are susceptible to becoming victims of outdated yet established cultural norms built upon erroneous masculine phenotypes that no longer serve to improve humanity.

Through all of this change and uncertainty, we have a tendency to go into protection mode. We think we are protecting ourselves when we remain shut down, when the reality is that layer of protection blocks us from living life. Trying to hide our wounds and be perfect just makes us less connected, maybe even harder to love. But learning a different way of operating takes some work and a newfound awareness; it's here where we see vulnerability naturally start to creep in. This willingness to be vulnerable is a sign of strength, and is the only way to the truth. When we're able to take our armor off and access the parts of our experience and psyche that are more fragile, that's when we can face off against the obstacles holding us back.

Real Men DO Cry

To take it a bit further with regard to men and the vulnerability game: Frankly, they get a bad rap, a bum deal, the shaft. Whatever you want to call it, they get screwed. Researcher and author Brené Brown, who I mentioned earlier, has studied vulnerability extensively, and in fact is considered the "queen of vulnerability," so she's kind of a big deal with this stuff. In my eyes, her in-depth research on shame and vulnerability is revolutionary and essential to our growth in interpersonal human relationships and development.

If you believe, like I do, that long-standing happiness and joy are achieved through cultivating deeper, more meaningful human relationships, then I would advise you to read Brown's work. Let me tell you a little bit about her. She holds a Ph.D. in social work and is a research professor at the University of Houston Graduate College of Social Work. She has spent more than 16 years studying vulnerability, courage, empathy and shame. Her book, *Daring Greatly*, has been next to my bed for years, and has changed my life. What makes Brown's work unique and inspiring is her refreshing combination of humorous, accessible dialogue coupled with well thought-out, proven research.

One aspect of her work I found particularly fascinating and courageous was the acknowledgement and validation of men and their experience with shame and vulnerability. And the realization that we women might be unconsciously sabotaging their efforts to be more vulnerable and sensitive. In *Daring Greatly*, she writes, "Basically men live under the pressure of one unrelenting message: Do not be perceived as weak." She goes on to talk about a man she met at one of her lectures several years ago who approached her and told her an honest, ugly truth: "My wife, and daughters—the ones you just signed all those books for—they'd rather see me die on top of my white horse than watch me fall off. You say you want us to be vulnerable and real, but c'mon. You can't stand it. It makes you sick to see us like that." WOW. Gulp. Eye-opening.

Ironically, many of the women she interviewed preached the benefits of a sensitive husband, that they all wanted one, yet the men she talked to reported that "the minute we start showing a crack, the reaction from our women is shame." Brown speaks of shame as a "fear of disconnection . . . it's the fear that something we have done or failed to do, an ideal that we've not lived up to, or a goal that we've not accomplished makes us unworthy of connection. I'm not worthy or good enough for love, belonging or connection. I'm unlovable. I don't belong."

See, we women have been programmed, too, and we have to break that cycle. We need to have the courage and self-worth and vulnerability to be proud of men who show their emotions, who cry and feel things. As mentioned at the beginning of this chapter, it's vital that we are in this together as men and women; it takes both genders to create the change we all seek.

And It Could Even Be a Matter of Life or Death. . .

To expand on male expectations and entrenched, outdated beliefs around feeling or being vulnerable, I recently came across a story reported by National Public Radio on an experiment done with oil rig workers in the Gulf of Mexico. Yes, this hits close to home, because I was born and raised in Houston, and my dad worked in the oil industry. Talk about tough men. These guys are paid to be tough. But they also faced the risk of death every day, and they never showed any vulnerability. This made their dangerous work even more perilous, because the men didn't ask for help and didn't dare admit if they weren't up to a certain job.

In 1997 Shell started building what would be the deepest offshore well in the world: Ursa, "vaster than anything they had ever attempted before." Rick Fox, the asset leader for Ursa, knew something had to change if it was going to be built and operated safely. He recognized that the men were not admitting their shortcomings, their lack of knowledge and information—because he saw it in himself. So he brought in Claire Nuer, a leadership consultant who was also a Holocaust survivor and New Age expert from California. She told Fox the men needed to deal with their feelings about seeing their friends die in brutal accidents, and their fears and insecurities about not being enough.

As the men learned more about themselves, they learned about each other, and they learned to trust. They changed. And they learned they could admit when they had a question if they didn't have all the information they needed to operate safely, and they wouldn't be chastised.

As a result, there was an 84 percent decline in Shell's accident rate. And because that image of the stony-faced, steely rig hand changed, not only did the men's performance soar, but their home lives got better, too. Fox himself reported that his relationship with his son improved, and the training gave him empathy for people he didn't even know, which made him a better manager. So, as much as we strive for that ideal to not appear weak because we fear any "crack" will expose us, it simply does not work—and quite frankly, it can be a matter of life and death.

I Cry at Work. There, I Said It

Feeling vulnerable crosses over to all aspects of our lives, and my career has been a breeding ground for teaching me about it. To be honest, your career is the first time in life that your parents can't really "fix" anything for you. It's all on you, and you're standing on wobbly legs that are liable to give out at any time. Again, I can't escape that "stomach becoming the size of a marble" feeling just thinking about my first job interview.

Early in my career, in the '90s, there was much less consciousness around issues of how to maintain your humanity in corporate situations. I was of the mind, like everyone else, that you had to compartmentalize, keep a stiff upper lip and no matter what happens, DON'T CRY AT WORK! And the fashion business can be brutal and erratic, to say the least.

One of my first jobs was working for a woman who didn't like me. It was the same woman I mentioned earlier who severely chastised me for being five minutes late to work. As a Leo, this is not something I'm innately prepared to deal with. One morning, she was getting down on me for something I did during a presentation. I started crying and she just looked at me in pure disgust. I went to the bathroom and the visions of my first attempt at varsity cheerleader came flooding back. But as embarrassed as I was feeling, I vividly remember having no shame. I remember thinking, *I am a human being, I have feelings and I am being mistreated.* I just knew in my gut it wasn't right. That was a big moment for me. I can still remember what I was wearing and what the bathroom stall looked like. I also knew I couldn't be who I really was in that job, so I looked for another one. Three months later I found one, left my current job and never looked back.

That moment illuminated for me that I had to maintain my humanness, and it also steered my management style at Elaine Turner. Obviously, professionalism is an attribute in the working world. You can't let your emotions run amok. But when we have difficult conversations (and we all have them) if there are tears—if you just found out your dad has cancer or you're going through a tough phase in a relationship—that emotion is valued. I never ask my employees to be anyone other than who they are. If it's a bad day, I'm going to honor that. Life is life. You don't have to be a robot or "act like a man." In fact, if you cry in front of me, there is a 99 percent chance I'll give you a high five and tell you I've been there, too.

Emotions don't make you weak. They make you human.

A lot of good work is done with emotion. Just think about marketing . . . what draws you in? Chances are it's something that is emotional, something that strikes a chord. Robots spouting out information just wouldn't do it for you. And robots just don't do it for me, either, in marketing or in my office.

Beyond my employees, my career has exposed me to many women wanting to share their stories and wounds, so when I give presentations I end up meeting people who want to connect with me for very different reasons than fashion. For example, I was in Louisiana last year giving a speech and doing a trunk show. There was a lovely young woman who waited in line to meet me and tell me about her young son, who had just been diagnosed with autism. We still email and share ideas about him to this day. So my career has been a gateway for me to meet people on a deeper level and share our stories, and it has been the fuel that has kept my engine burning when I've wanted to just shut down. Every person I come across, every life I touch, every hand I shake, every tear I shed, every person I hug . . . this is my legacy. This is who I am.

A Woman's Greatest Battle Is With Herself

We women are perfectionists. We people-please. We believe in the big myth taught to us at a young age: If you're "good enough," it all works out in the end. We play many roles wearing many hats, all while suffocating under the illusion we can do it all and be it all. Misguided, often unrealistic expectations are placed on us as we seemingly glide through the overwhelming demands of everyday life. We accept those expectations and break our necks trying to be perfect all the time. And when we're not, we lose it (picture the breast pump smashing against the wall).

Research states that the top two areas for women of not feeling good enough are in relation to **how we look** and **how we parent**. Unfortunately, women are held up to impossible standards: Stay feminine, sweet, thin and modest, and make it all look easy. I'm going to quote Brené Brown here again; she just has such good shit to say about perfectionism, so stay with me.

Brown eloquently states, "The real struggle for women—what amplifies shame regardless of the category—is that we're expected (and sometimes desire) to be perfect, yet we're not allowed to look as if we're working for it." She defines it as "women and the shame web." She uses a cobweb as a metaphor describing how when we attempt to be everything to everyone, it only ensnares us tighter in an inescapable, sticky spider web of becoming more and more stuck. She references the classic double-blind scenario where all your options are limited and all of them expose you to penalty; in essence it's a no-win scenario.

How many times have you felt that way? No matter how much you do or how much you hustle, you still feel like it isn't enough. The reality is we are human. Men and women alike. For instance, I know I'm aging: My hair is graying, my mind is tired, my body is swollen and no matter how many omega-3s I swallow, I still feel puffy.

Thank God for Spanx, caftans, yoga pants and the color black, because there are some things kale and coconut oil just can't solve. But why, oh why, do we do this to ourselves? It creates unsustainable, even detrimental conditions to exist within.

Colbie Caillat is one of my favorite recording artists. I listen to her all the time while fast-walking, putting on my makeup, sleeping on an airplane—she's my girl. She wrote a song a couple of years ago that had a huge impact on me. Every time I think I'm not good enough, sexy enough, thin enough, I think about this song. She titled it "Try." This song speaks to me on so many levels. It confronts the issues of people pleasing and hustling toward perfectionism head-on, and releases us from feeling the need to change who we are to feel worthy. I especially love the line she slips in, "Do you like you?"—because that's all that matters anyway. As far as I can tell, self-love is the real arbiter of true happiness.

And like looking good isn't enough pressure, there's that whole other area where we continue to feel "less than": parenting. While there are plenty of women who don't have children and are perfectionists, there's nothing quite as intense as a mom who feels the pressure to be perfect and to be . . .

. . . a GOOD mother. (Gulp.) Yep, I said it.

Chances are those standards we hold up for ourselves as mothers come from the outside: from society; from our family, friends and acquaintances; from television, movies and books. Basically, from what we've been taught are "good mom" traits . . . and we have no doubt pinned them on Pinterest for quick reference. And from what I can see, those traits create the dreaded, never-ending "should," "always" and "never" word-vomit loop that gets stuck on repeat in our heads:

Always be happy.
Always listen to your baby.
You should exclusively breastfeed your baby.
You should stay home with your baby.
Always be patient with your child.
Never miss the important events.
Always be consistent.

You know what I think? Being a mother doesn't suddenly require perfection—if anything, it requires humanity, modeling for our kids that not everything is always picture-perfect, but that doesn't mean it's not awesome (or, shall we say, good enough). And just as important as allowing yourself the room to not be the world's best mother is letting your kids see you f* up. As I'm writing this, I was supposed to go to a college visit with my son, Harrison. Well, against my Pinterest board's guidance, it didn't happen. I didn't get to check off everything on the list of "Top 10 things you should do with your kid on their 2,380th college visit." Wanna know why? I'm too damn tired from a workweek full of public speaking obligations and I'm on a deadline to finish this book. So instead of forcing something that wasn't fitting, I called him and told him the truth. I cringed awaiting his response . . . which was "Mom, don't worry about it, you don't have to always try to be the perfect mother." He went with his dad instead and, you guessed it, we all survived.

I think it's imperative to show your child that you are not perfect. Show them you can make mistakes, and that you can work to correct them. That you can yell and maybe even hurt someone's feelings, and you can apologize because you are truly sorry. Your children will still love you, and they will learn it's possible to love someone who is imperfect, and thank God for that. And then they can grow up to be imperfect and love someone who is imperfect, instead of holding themselves and everyone around them to a Pinterest-level standard of perfection.

Family Lessons

One of my biggest and most influential lessons in accessing my vulnerability started with watching my parents and how they raised us. Our parents were the nucleus of our family. They were the strong foundation on which we were built, and if I'm honest, I think their children arrived to test their strength. They were given deep, complicated children and they've done their best to raise us well. But the bottom line is my parents were never believers in the idea that all children should be treated the same way, or that it was somehow unfair for a child to receive more or less attention from a parent. They had three distinctly different children, and they celebrated all three of us with the same vigor and belief as if we were each their only child. They believed all children should get what they need, and what they need depends on who they are as individuals. For them, it was never about what was fair or unfair; it was always about need. Simply put, if you needed more, you got more. I have carried this wisdom with me in how I parent today; thank God for it because my children are vastly dissimilar with entirely different needs.

I know I've mentioned this before, but I'm discovering that the best teacher in my life, thus far, is my daughter, Marlie. She has been and is my most consequential gateway toward becoming the best version of myself. She has taught me how to feel in a new, transcendental way, and how to be OK with the ups and downs. I have always had what feels like immediate access to vulnerability, but she has allowed me to enter something that feels like an invitation-only poker ring—a lot of rough-around-the-edges moments, along with cursing, laughing and big emotional payouts.

If I'm honest, Marlie is the impetus for all the work I'm doing now with my writing and serving others through sharing my story. Every single moment I'm engaged with her, I access a part of myself that is wholehearted and compassionate, coming from a place of humanity. Validating her challenges and where she is, rather than trying to make her someone she cannot be, has strengthened my compassion to a level I'm not even sure I can articulate. I trust and validate Marlie when things are hard for her. There is a very sensitive balance that Jim and I are trying to keep with her. We're not trying to make her what she cannot become, but we also don't ever want to underestimate what she can do or be. The greatest challenge in raising her is deciding when to push her out of her comfort zone and when to accept she's not ready. Knowing when to bluff and when to show all our cards, but also knowing when it's time to back off and allow us all a chance to retreat. Our greatest fear is creating a sense of learned helplessness in her, so we are continually nudging her toward knowing she can do it.

When I find myself in this internal conflict, I try to access my intuition and see if anything comes up. It's amazing what creating a little space can do in finding the answers. Through all of this, I've learned a great deal about acceptance, letting go and meeting her right where she is rather than where I think she could or should be. My role in being a mother to Marlie has been my most challenging journey of all, but it also has been my greatest opportunity to evolve, grow, learn and, most importantly, to LOVE.

An example of this type of unconditional love happened about a year and a half ago when Marlie was enrolled in a school for high-functioning autistic children. Many of her peers at the time were diagnosed with Asperger's Syndrome and even though social interaction proved to be challenging, many of them performed well in school. In contrast, Marlie's challenges are the other way around. She actually does pretty well socially but academics are a nightmare for her. Marlie was quickly becoming aware of her differences and feeling less and less confident.

As the year progressed, Marlie began to struggle even more. Every morning, she was refusing to go to school, and was having frequent anxiety attacks. I could see her emotionally begin to shut down. We were doing all we could and meeting with her therapist multiple times a week. We attempted to create coping strategies we felt could work for her, but in the end, we were unsuccessful.

Jim and I were devastated. We were not sure what to do or where to go next. And right about that the same time, my mother-in-law suddenly died of a stroke. Needless to say, we were shocked, grief stricken and paralyzed. Our daughter was refusing to go to school and now we were dealing with a serious, unexpected tragedy. It was the worst time of my life. Almost unbearable. Shortly after Jim's mother's funeral, we pulled Marlie out of school and decided to keep her at home until we knew what next step to take. Our family was heart broken.

As much as I was resistant to the idea of her not going to school, I also knew that this was our new reality. As time moved on, I could see Marlie take comfort in being at home and taking a break. I began to open up to new ideas and explored several alternative avenues for her education. I realized that maybe Marlie held all the answers. She knew all along what was right for her. Even though her communication skills are limited, she was doing all she could to tell us she was unhappy and needed a new environment. I knew I had to trust her and have faith that we would find the right situation moving forward. It was an incredibly difficult time, but I found strength in trusting my daughter. I knew this wasn't just a matter of defiance or a classic case of separation anxiety, this was a fundamental shift in her behavior telling us: I CAN'T GO TO THIS SCHOOL ANY LONGER.

Long story short, Marlie took about 9 months off from school. I like to say we hit a reset button. Today she is happily enrolled in a new school that has turned out to be the perfect fit. It's truly a miracle for our family, We struggled and struggled for so many years to find the right situation for Marlie and we finally have. I still pinch myself every morning dropping her off, knowing she is finally at peace with where she is, but more importantly, I look at my daughter and recognize and acknowledge that she knows exactly what is right for her. The moral of the story is . . . Marlie knew all along what she needed and all Jim and I needed to do was TRUST HER. Listen to your kids. Trust their words. Trust their actions. They are trying to tell you something so stop, listen and love them through it.

With regard to our son, Harrison, it's a different ball game. My son knows we aren't defined by the precariousness of the scarcity culture that surrounds us where "nothing is enough," e.g., no ACT score is high enough, no college is elite enough. No, not us—we are defined by our humanity. I believe we are not human beings living a spiritual life; we are spiritual beings living a human life. I tell him that all that time. I confess, he looks at me funny, but that's OK. One day it will sink in.

Harrison's path has been a more mainstream experience—whatever that means—so we are dealing with a different set of issues with him. In some ways, we are typical. We're talking about the usual teenage stuff that most households across the U.S. are talking about: responsibility around drinking, limiting social media use, peer pressure, etc. But Harry isn't living in a "normal" household; he's living in a household with two working parents and a special needs sister. I know for him, it has been a long, arduous, slow burn toward understanding the truth, but the truth has already set him free. I see it every day. I see him freely and willingly access his empathy and compassion, even when it feels hard to do. I see his patience fully developed when it comes to the unpredictable emotions or behaviors that often arise. I see his loyalty and commitment to Marlie, even when others have walked away and given up. But most of all, I see him offer his pure, raw, unconditional love to her.

Harrison has shown up in all ways. He helps me regulate Marlie's social media use and is the first to call or text me when he feels she might be compromised or exploited. He goes to every annual pediatrician appointment with her to support her on any new vaccinations that are needed. He even has had his teeth drilled in front of her to show her how "it isn't really that big of a deal," and if he can do it, so can she. He includes her when his friends show up to play Fortnight so she can watch and cheer them all on. I'm embarrassed to admit this last one, but he even attended her year-end award ceremony at school this year with his dad because I was out of town. He immediately called me afterward with pure excitement in his voice to tell me about all the awards she won. Harrison is our blessing. He's our gift. Their relationship reminds me of the lyrics in my favorite U2 song, "One": "One life with each other, sisters, brothers, one life, but we're not the same, we get to carry each other, carry each other, one, one . . ."

Keeping Up With the Joneses (Not!)

Over the years, I've found that embracing your family's authentic self can almost be more of an emotionally vulnerable journey than embracing your own self. With family, the mama bear instinct kicks in and your sole purpose is to protect. Being vulnerable opens us up and makes us completely raw—it puts our tender hearts out on display and we go from feeling like a grizzly bear to a Build-

A-Bear. For most people, it's terrifying to be so open and honest about our "shortcomings," nonconformity or differences, but it's also so freeing to feel the weight of the showboating world lift off of your shoulders. From the littlest of things, like the cheese ball I bring (and will continue to bring) to all family gatherings and make zero effort to hide the Kroger wrapper (mama bear don't cook) to the out-of-our control challenges like Marlie's genetic condition, we all have areas of our life that are in discord with what the world tells us is "OK." When we found out about Marlie's genetic condition, we kept it close to the vest in an effort to guard our hearts—and honestly to also "protect" how people viewed us and our daughter—but as we have had the time to digest our reality, I have found so much strength in it. I have found power in accepting that we are our own Joneses and the only responsibility we have is to keep up with our true selves. To fight every day for what we love, who we love and how we love. That might mean an uncomfortable moment or two, but f* it. My life is crazy, and I'd drive myself crazy trying to hide it for the sake of others.

I once read that "a good family is a family that keeps trying." I love that. It's true. Once you stop trying, indifference sets in, and indifference breeds disengagement. Make no mistake, we don't pretend to be the best at hosting Thanksgiving dinner or going to church on a regular basis or not cussing at each other or always having all the right answers. We are simply human beings on this journey together, and pretending we can walk this walk flawlessly is a recipe for unhappiness. So, at the Turners', mistakes are welcomed (even celebrated), bumps are expected, plateaus are embraced and perfectionism is denied at the front door. But ***love*** is essential.

As a family, we try hard to remain focused on what's important. Our family values aren't based around society's dictations or our achievements. The truth is every family has their own set of values. And rightfully so. The answers to what we value and what we deem important are different for everyone. But what is important is to attempt to define what you value and then collectively move toward it. What's scary about some families today is there seems to be a binary view of being either achievement-based or survival-based.

In my eyes, there's no black-or-white way of raising your children; even when you think there is—there isn't. Life doesn't work that way. In some ways, having a special needs daughter has freed me from the notions that it all has to be and look a certain way. Of course I would have chosen for her to never have suffered with challenges, but when you allow grace and acceptance to flow in, it's amazing how liberating it can be. When you stop being in resistance to what's real, things begin to open up. When you accept that the universe is exactly as it should be, life becomes more clear, the truth becomes sweeter and the pain is transformed into something beautiful. I know my case is more extreme than most. Most of us aren't living with children or adults with special needs, but let's say you are dealing with a child with mild learning differences, or a child who is introverted and never gets invited to the party, or a child with a pretty serious case of ADHD who has behavioral issues and causes problems at school. Try to imagine letting go of wanting the situation to change. Instead, try to imagine your resistance to it subsiding. Try to see it for what it is. All of a sudden you will see the light shine through and it won't appear the same. They say nothing changes unless YOU do, so change the way you view, react and engage with the challenges you are presented with. A change WITHIN you is powerful enough to change the world AROUND you. Maya Angelou once said, "Try to change the world around you. If you can't, change your attitude."

In our family, we don't place a lot of value on being like everyone else. That ship sailed at birth. And when I say that, what I mean is at our house it's OK to not get invited, it's OK to not go to the same church as all of our neighbors, it's OK to be different, it's OK to be authentic without apology. In some ways, we almost take pride in it.

I am a big believer that while on this earth, one of the most fundamental tools you can possess is having the ability to stand alone, because when you have the courage to stand for what's right even when you're on your own, it builds character. And strong character eventually attracts the right tribe. So, if you can withstand the temporary loneliness of feeling or being alone, I promise you will one day reap the benefits and blessings of a shared common bond with likeminded souls who are all waiting patiently to cross your divine road map. And guess what? You won't have to fake anything in front of these people because you stood alone to find them.

So, as I say to my 18-year-old impressionable son, stand alone in your college choice, stand alone hanging out with someone in the "wrong" friend group, stand alone in taking a class that not one of your close friends would dare take, stand alone in opting out of lacrosse to focus on your incredible writing skills, stand alone in including your special needs sister in everything you do and not giving a shit about what your "cool" friends think.

Stand alone, my friend. Don't get lost in a sea of Joneses.

Beautifully Broken

Now that we have explored the topic of vulnerability, I don't know about you, but I feel a little cracked open. As Rumi said, "The wound is the place where the light enters you," and being vulnerable and accessing our wounds allows us to fully engage with our brokenness. When I say brokenness, I mean that sacred part of ourselves that has faced the entire spectrum of life's experiences, from the positive and uplifting to the damning and heartbreaking. If you are, in fact, human, it's probably safe to say your life up to this point has had some pain mixed in, and as human beings living human lives, our wholeness MUST include the acceptance of our brokenness.

This whole idea of brokenness reminds me of my love for older homes. Have you ever walked into an older home and been astonished by its beauty? Something about its age, history and beautiful *brokenness* attracted you. Honoring the past, honoring the wear and tear, honoring the souls who once lived there. It's as if you feel a part of something deeply rooted in the past, something created by our shared human experiences and the lives we spend a lifetime building. I've been in homes where I could almost feel the souls who have lived there before; I could sense the love between family members and the hardship of what old age brings. These homes held a sacred contradiction of being both perfectly whole and perfectly broken at the same time. Just as human beings, we cannot be whole without being broken. But it's here, in this place of brokenness, where the light shines through. It's here where we can choose to either shut down, close ourselves off, or join together and find healing in our shared wounds.

It's like the woman I mentioned earlier whom I met in Louisiana—she made a choice that day. She made a choice to share, to step up and expose herself to the unknown. She made a choice to connect with me over our shared hardship of both having children with neurological disorders. Imagine how much better the world would be if we could see the beauty in the places we have been broken. If our brokenness inspires us to transform our pain into something positive, if our brokenness inspires our creativity and productivity, if our brokenness valiantly tells our authentic story, both the good and not-so-good parts, then why pretend we're perfect and without flaws? The human experience is messy and imperfect because it's meant to be. We are here to learn and experience our full range of emotions and share our wounds in order to heal one another.

You see, a funny thing happens when you begin to witness and share your own pain: It begins to work for you. As I mentioned in the introduction, when your pain feels truly seen, it wants to transmute itself into something beautiful and productive. In your art of feeling, you are more easily able to find your truth and your mission.

And isn't this why we are all here?

ASK YOURSELF

Allowing yourself to be vulnerable and also show it, is a sign of strength and truly a path to awareness and enlightenment. Open up to these questions.

1. **What wounds are you afraid of showing to your friends, your colleague or boss?** What do you think would happen if you did? Write them down, and also write your worst fantasy about them. Are those fantasies realistic?

2. **Do you feel you are "oversensitive"?** Why? Has someone told you that you take things too seriously or feel things too strongly? Maybe they are afraid of their own emotions and vulnerabilities. See if you can imagine asking them what is so bad about showing your feelings (or maybe you can really ask them). Take note of their answers.
3. **How do you handle stress?** When something negative happens at work, what do you do? Do you blame yourself or try to find someone else to blame? What happens when you are angry at a loved one? Do you hold grudges? All of these questions can reveal your feelings around vulnerability and how well you maintain your balance of mind and emotion.

* * *

Chapter 5

MYTH: OUR FAILURES DEFINE US

"Life's a bitch and then you die . . ."

. . . as my no-nonsense grandmother would often say. Sounds aggressive, but it's true. Anita was her name, and to say she had a spitfire personality is putting it lightly. She was known for her matter-of-fact opinions, crusty comebacks and no-holds-barred outlook on life. She might not have been for everyone, but she was a breath of fresh air to me.

Once you got past her sharp edges, a softness emerged. She loved like no one I have ever known. The kind of love you can only feel, not explain. Her love ran so deep that she became irrational at the slightest dig of someone she adored. I was held tight to her heart and I prayed for the soul who would even ever so slightly question my capabilities to her. I guess I, too, got the gift (or curse) of having no filter—thanks, Grandma.

But really, the confidence I have? It's from her. She was my biggest fan. I can remember her sitting in her lawn chair with her visor on, smoking a cigarette, watching me at all my swim meets and tennis tournaments. She really was the best kind of fan to have. Regardless of my wins or losses, my grandma thought I was the bomb. If I couldn't beat 'em on the tennis court, she would inevitably point out that I was cuter, had better legs and wore a prettier outfit. I guess you could say she had a way of putting me in the winner's circle every day. My parents' job was to guide me, constructively criticize and mitigate any further disappointments as only true parents can do, but my grandma's job was to simply LOVE me.

If anyone taught me it was OK to f* up, it was her—and thank God for it.

In fact, I've been thinking a lot about her lately and what she would be advising me to do if she were still here today. You see, I'm currently smack dab in the eye of a "failure" shitstorm. I am being forced to face some harsh truths and new realities surrounding my brick-and-mortar retail business, and quite frankly, it sucks. You know, the revolutionary type of suckage . . . like when United Airlines bought out Continental, and we've all been subjected to flying the "not-so-friendly skies" ever since. That type of suck.

We are in the process of shutting down several of our underperforming retail stores due to a volatile retail market in which it feels like consumer shopping behaviors are changing faster than the speed of light. And if I'm honest, it feels a lot like failure to me.

As an entrepreneur I have seen a lot of sides of myself—even sides I'd rather ignore. Being an entrepreneur is like standing in one of those dressing rooms with mirrors all around you that duplicate you into oblivion. It takes away the ability to ignore the stuff you hate, the cellulite, the irrational decisions, the moments of weakness and the very potent reality of failure.

Two Rocks, a Spark, and a NEW Era

I read somewhere that becoming a successful entrepreneur is like trying to start a fire with two rocks. You can bang those rocks together for years and fail at creating anything, but you only need one spark to create a fire. Well, I've been banging and banging and banging rocks (not my husband, much to his dismay) for more than 18 years now, and I've been fortunate enough to create some roaring fires, yet right now, all my banging isn't igniting the sparks needed to thrive in this new era of retail and consumerism. I'm at a difficult crossroads, calling me to change, to find a new direction, a new reality, a new beginning. And that new beginning is requiring me to close stores.

I can't lie—I feel like I've been ousted by the popular crowd and subjected to eating my feelings with my new best friend: Failure. She has bad breath, and even worse jokes. She stares at me waiting for answers to her incessant questions, and demands that I carry all her baggage. I kinda hate her and I need her to go away. I'm hoping by writing this chapter, she will release the stronghold she has on my psyche of feeling like I'm a big, fat failure and not good enough. (Brené, where are you when I need you?) She's a clingy bitch, too. It's all a little suffocating.

Failure . . . or Shall We Say "Perceived Failure"?

As much as I hate my "frenemy," Failure, I've come to terms with her. To be honest, it's taken years of work and a lot of business strategy to realize that Failure is more of an imaginary friend (maybe the bad breath is mine?! . . . mental note to get breath mints). She only has as much power as I give her.

How we decide to see failure usually goes back to what society has dictated to us about what it looks like. And it's subjective, just as success is. Actually, I don't believe in failure. I prefer the term "**perceived failure**." Ultimately, it's how we choose to look at what happens to us that's important. We might perceive we have failed, but have we? Or are we still learning, course-correcting, evolving, growing and taking the necessary steps to get to where we want to be? Is the universe actually setting us up for our true purpose? The journey between your questions and your answers is life; it's the journey that propels you. The questions allow you to look at things from a different angle. As you shift your focus, you shift your possibilities.

How Low Can You Go?

I've had to do a lot of shifting and angle changes to find the new way forward for my company. For the past several months, my angle has been on the floor, feeling a little steamrolled by life. I've mustered up the courage to roll over and look up to the sky for answers. This new perspective has allowed me the ability to look beyond my current situation and see the infinite possibilities. I've found that the only time we are bound by our perceived failures is when we let them paralyze us. If we can keep shifting focus and angles, we can find answers, and I think, I pray, I've found mine.

I've come up with a new strategy. It is indeed my boldest move yet: to provide our customers with every opportunity imaginable to find beauty, connection, philanthropy and fashion on their own terms and in their own way, with us by their side, just as we've always been.

The retail landscape has changed. We are seeing firsthand that consumers want to engage with luxury brands in a personal way across multiple platforms, in varying places and at a pace that changes constantly. Over the past several years, the walls between sales channels have slowly disappeared, and we are empowering our customers to participate in a way that works for them.

Our goal is to serve our customer in an innovative way. With the recent emergence of the "Amazon Age" taking over retail, ease, convenience and speed are at the center of most transactions. Consumers are demanding an original, more customized way to shop. They're smarter, savvier and busier than ever, any way they want to engage with the brand we must make it happen.

The idea is to provide a few ways to do it. If she likes to shop by the click of a button, she can visit ElaineTurner.com. If she is involved in her community, we will host a Glamorous Giving Charity Party in one of our remaining flagship stores. If she just had a vampire facial and needs a few days to recover (and not scare people), we can bring fashion to her through our newly launched suite of concierge services: our nationwide elite stylists or the Elaine Turner Edit customized box program. You know, a box program. You tell us about your style, we put together a box based on the info you give us. We curate and send you what we think you'll like. If you like, you keep; if not, you send back. Easy-peasy. Try before you buy. And for all those non-shoppers out there, the box will be like your new best friend, arriving at your front door unannounced with goodies on hand. All you need now is your favorite bottle of wine and a good mirror to get the night going.

I'm excited about the new possibilities, but I had to endure bruises (ego included) to push me to a place of problem-solving. Like I said before, we are only as stuck as we let ourselves believe. I hope I have managed to get my company unstuck (and I hope my bad back allows me to get up off the floor).

Some of the Best Were Once the Worst

Let's just say it: **For the most part, life is about falling on your ass**. But I firmly believe failure can be a gateway to awareness, and an opportunity to learn and grow and be even better than before. So maybe it's all about failure bringing us one step closer to success (or to whatever we perceive to be success).

Truth be told, you usually have to fail to succeed. No one simply arrives at the top. Even when it seems someone has it all together and has never tasted the bitterness of failure, if you dig deep enough and peel back the layers, there is usually more to the story. A story which includes some bad luck, setbacks, unforeseen circumstances and flat out failures.

For example, we all know the legendary stories of people we admire who have presumably failed miserably. Steve Jobs was fired by the company he co-founded. Yet it was during this period of exile that he picked up a little computer graphics company. You may have heard of it: Pixar Animation Studios. The sale of this company made him a billionaire.

Thomas Edison failed 1,000 times before creating the light bulb, Stephen King's first novel was rejected 30 times and Henry Ford failed at starting several automotive companies before starting Ford Motor Company.

And then, there is my favorite, Abraham Lincoln. He is probably the single greatest example of someone who has failed and failed A LOT throughout his lifetime. But guess what? He never quit. He might have adapted his plan or changed his course, but he never, ever threw in the towel. He continued to get back up each day and begin again, even with all that he was up against.

Born into poverty, Lincoln was faced with defeat throughout his life. He lost eight elections, twice failed in business and suffered a nervous breakdown (hey, me too!). He could have quit many times, but he didn't. And because he didn't quit, he became one of the greatest presidents in the history of our country. Lincoln truly exemplifies what it means to get yourself back up after you stumble.

I guess the moral of the story is you need to be prepared to lose (a lot) before you really start winning. Failing over and over again can be discouraging; it's the reason most successful people I know are mentally strong, and maybe a little insane. For instance, my father is one of the most mentally tough (mildly insane) people I know. Throughout his career in the oil industry, he navigated Houston's boom or bust economy with courage. Instead of playing it safe in difficult times, he did the opposite. He looked for the opportunity. As I've aged and gone through my own career ups and downs, he's shared with me the reality of those times. One time I remember him telling me how important it was to take risks and be bold in times of change. And these words of wisdom have stuck with me today. I attempt to look at my situation with our stores as an opportunity to serve my customers in a new way instead of giving up.

As mentioned, I've also suffered a lot of failure and challenges in my life, and I can honestly say the single biggest take away from all of it is coming to understand how strong I really am. If there is anything failure has taught me, it's that I am a survivor. And, speaking of survival, I am obsessed with J.K. Rowling. Not only am I a huge Harry Potter fan (Gryffindor, anyone?), but I also love her other works. I am inspired by her story and everything she has overcome to get to where she is today. She wrote the most amazing commencement address for the Harvard 2008 graduation. Her speech was made into a book, which I gave to my 18-year-old son. He's graduating from high school this year, so I thought some of it might resonate with him. I tend to quote it often, which triggers quite a few eye rolls around the kitchen table, but I'm immune to caring about eye rolls at this point.

One of the main topics Rowling addressed in her speech was *failure*. She said, "The knowledge that you have emerged wiser and stronger from setbacks means that you are, ever after, secure in your ability to survive. You will never truly know yourself, or the strength of your relationships, until both have been tested by adversity. Such knowledge is a true gift, for all that it is painfully won, and it has been worth more than any qualification I ever earned." Can I get an Amen?

Easing Into a Fearless Mindset

Approaching life willing to learn from your mistakes or your perceived failures takes audacity, bravery and courage. It takes saying yes to taking risks, living a remarkable life and falling down, to continue pushing hard and staying in the game, and then having the awareness to look at what happened if you lose. If you ski or surf, or invest, or even date, you know the saying: If you don't wipe out, lose money or get rejected, you aren't trying hard enough. They say to fail is to be human. But to resurrect oneself is an act of courage.

Some big thinkers call this GRIT.

I started becoming interested in the idea of grit after reading Angela Duckworth's book *Grit: The Power of Passion and Perseverance.* She is a Harvard grad and MacArthur "genius" grant winner, and has become an expert in researching and studying the power of developing grit. She describes grit as a combination of passion and perseverance for a singularly important goal. She is convinced that it is the hallmark of high achievers in every domain, and has also found scientific evidence that grit can actually *grow* over time.

Duckworth researched teachers working in some of the country's roughest schools, West Point cadets and finalists in the National Spelling Bee. What she found was that "One characteristic emerged as a significant predictor of success. And it wasn't social intelligence. It wasn't good looks, physical health, and it wasn't IQ. It was grit." Passion and perseverance.

A recent study found that the fear of failing plagued 31 percent of adult respondents, a larger percentage than those who feared spiders (30 percent), being home alone (9 percent) or even the paranormal (15 percent).*

**latimes.com/health/la-he-scared-20151031-story.html*

Time to buck up and go beyond that fear: When we fail, we learn, we grow and we mature. If we are brave enough, we can achieve new understandings and perspectives on life, love, business, money, relationships and people. It opens our eyes to new pathways toward reaching our goals and connecting the dots where we hadn't before.

We need to understand that the failures we are continually learning from are laying the foundation to win later. As James Joyce said, "Mistakes are the portal of discovery." And come on, if you fail, at least you had the balls to try. If you really want something, you have to be willing to fail to get it. And that's how I am trying to see my current situation with the stores. If I want to continue to build a great company, I need to face my fear and do the hard, right thing in order to get there. Even if it means I am not going to have an enormous fleet of retail stores.

I'm a believer that failure and defeat are life's greatest teachers, but sadly, most people don't want to go there. I, on the other hand, am not in a position, nor do I have the luxury, to quietly sit under the radar while the marketplace continues to move forward without me. I must and will act. I have to walk straight through the pain cloud and fail, if that's what going to happen. This goes against what our society so dearly preserves, the "success at all costs" mantra. However, in my company I am preaching the opposite.

I'm saying that great success depends on great risk, and failure is simply a common by-product. We cannot wallow in our mistakes, but instead must parlay them into future gains. We must adapt, and have the courage to innovate. We have to develop an attitude toward failure of "No Fear." We have to be willing to stick our necks out and join in the conversation of how to use our key differentiators to our best advantage. We need to be risky and fearless in how we execute and implement plans and ideas. And most importantly, we cannot be afraid of rejection or failure in the process.

The same holds true personally—achieving your personal best takes a change in mindset. It takes finding the light deep inside of you that knows it can and will overcome and not getting stuck in the negative self-talk loop that so often accompanies failure. For me, I've noticed one of my biggest daily challenges with overcoming hardship is not allowing myself to become the problem. If we aren't careful, we can become our burdens. A new, unhealthy dynamic starts to form within yourself where your identity and thought process begin to change toward the negative. It's as if we cannot see ourselves outside of our failures. That's dangerous. Our failures are not us. We cannot become defined by them. They are simply life's way of pushing us to grow and find a new way forward.

No matter what area you perceive yourself to be failing in, one of the best qualities we can learn for ourselves, and teach our children, is the ability to accept failure as a reality in life and to learn to build resilience.

Our society spends so much time avoiding failure that we are unintentionally undermining a very essential life skill: the ability to get yourself back up after a fall. Whatever you want to call it—grit, resiliency, a stiff upper lip, a pick-yourself-up-by-your-bootstraps mindset or perseverance—essentially, it's all we've got. We can't control life, so our best tool to combat that lack of control is to build these qualities within ourselves so we are better able to handle what life throws our way.

Turning Failure Into Success

We've all heard the old adage that repeating the same task while expecting a different result is the definition of insanity. In essence, failing is only beneficial if you learn from your experiences and adapt and modify your behavior. You could also say that failing to learn from your failures is failing in the literal sense of the word.

The best way to turn failure into success is to take time to analyze your failure and see what went wrong and what went right. Make a clear assessment of your level of competence in the areas needed for success. Re-evaluate your plan, preparation and execution. Discover what went wrong and do your best to fix it. As Malcolm Forbes once said, "Failure is success if we learn from it."

So let's do this thing. The great news is, there are some wonderful payoffs.

1. Failure makes us stronger

Failure taps into our ability to overcome and survive. Just like J.K. Rowling said, surviving failure at the very least teaches us that you "are, ever after, secure in your ability to survive." I can honestly say the one thing I always walk away with when things are extremely difficult in my life is the belief and discovery about myself that I am stronger than I think I am. There is something extremely healing about validating and recognizing your own strength and your capacity to recover from setbacks. This knowing is almost primal in nature; it ensures our capacity to continue to fight the good fight.

2. Failure sparks a change in direction

Failure can be the spark that ignites change. We can either go down the road of despair or chart a new beginning. In my case, I'm choosing to see it as an opportunity to grow and become even better. I believe we can empower ourselves by knowing that what grows out of the initial failure is entirely up to us.

Don't get me wrong, it's easy, even natural to become depressed, bitter and suffer with low self esteem when things don't go as planned. And I think it's perfectly OK to feel these emotions. Go ahead, feel your disappointment fully, and then, when you are ready, channel it into something that can work for you. Attempt to use the failure to your advantage. It could be a time for reinvention or a modest course correction, but whatever it is, choose to see as a chance to move in a new, much needed direction.

3. Failure tames the ego

With all the over-the-top media exposure and larger-than-life imagery at our fingertips 24/7, we begin to believe in fairy tales. As a result, remaining down-to-earth in today's world can be challenging. Society tells us that more is definitely better and enough is never really enough—never enough money, never enough fame, never enough stuff . . . you name it, I'll bet you think you need more of it.

Many who experience high levels of outward success tend to become addicted by its illusory draw. They become mesmerized by materialistic consumption and the perceived power it brings. When this happens, and I know we have all seen it, a certain form of desperation can set in, and they will go to any length to retain it. People resort to dishonesty and become slaves to success, and before realizing it, they'll do anything to stay on top, even things they would never have imagined. With this ego driven behavior comes turmoil. Business partnerships and even friendships are ruined. Family conflicts abound. It's all downhill from there, even if their bank account remains full. And that, too, will inevitably dwindle. Failure brings us humility and humility is what's so often needed when the ego is left unchecked. It humanizes us when we start to feel more powerful than we should. It helps us remember where we came from, keeps us grounded and brings us back to our true nature.

4. Failure creates "aha" moments of awareness

When we perceive we have failed, it's essential to bring awareness to the situation so we can grow from it instead of just staying in reaction mode. Failure has the potential to create: the "aha" moment. For instance, as my store business began to suffer, I had many "aha" moments around what I could do differently to improve my business. It was up to me to tune in and adapt and react to the problem at hand. It's tempting to just move on to the next thing without really thinking about what you could do differently or how you could learn from what happened. In my case, our awareness was heightened and we could react with growth and innovation. If we are disengaged, we miss the opportunity to restrategize, fix and ultimately save ourselves.

5. Failure clarifies what we prioritize and value

When you perceive yourself to have failed, something unexpected happens. You begin to redefine your priorities in life. Everything becomes more clear and you begin to reorder the things that matter to you. You look inward and do the self work it takes to discover the things that matter most to you. This, my friends, is probably the single most important by-product. There is nothing more important in life than gaining clarity around what's essential. When this happens, everything else naturally begins to slough off, creating a grace-filled spotlight on the people you love and the things you treasure.

Again, as J.K. Rowling said so perfectly in her Harvard commencement speech: "So why do I talk about the benefits of failure? Simply because failure meant a stripping away of the inessential. I stopped pretending to myself that I was anything other than what I was, and began to direct all my energy into finishing the only work that mattered to me. Had I really succeeded at anything else, I might never have found the determination to succeed in the one arena I believed I truly belonged. I was set free, because my greatest fear had been realized, and I was still alive, and I still had a daughter whom I adored, and I had an old typewriter and a big idea. And so rock bottom became the solid foundation on which I rebuilt my life." (Note: Rowling had just gone through a divorce, didn't have a job or much money. That idea, of course, was for Harry Potter.)

Many of the values in my life have been reshaped. What I valued 10 years ago is not what I value today. That may also be true for you. When people are struggling to succeed, it could be a sign they have their values in the wrong places. Perceived flops, especially ones that you keep repeating, force you to look at the goals you've set. Maybe they aren't really right for you today.

6. Failure brings forth compassion

The way I see it, we are all only one bad decision or unfortunate circumstance away from feeling extreme failure. This understanding brings forth the realization of just how human we really are and how we are more alike than unalike. Failure tends to crack the ego, and as a result, you become more compassionate, more empathetic and more in touch with your fellow human beings. It forces you to look deeper at things, understanding and caring more about others rather than solely focusing on yourself.

This empathetic compassion has "motherhood" written all over it. We've all been there. Kidless, standing in a checkout line watching some poor mother deal with a Candygate situation with her heathen, shoeless child in the next aisle over. We stare in disgust and lie to ourselves, thinking, *My kid will never act like that* or *I will never give in to the every whim of my child to avoid a public outburst. Oh, and they won't stay up late, they won't disrespect me, piss on the floor or shun vegetables.* Blah blah blah.

Motherhood is nothing if not humbling. All the perfect things you had envisioned in your mind—white sofas, breakables within arm's reach, sweet clean playrooms, Jenny Lind beds, princess dresses—will get barfed on, shit on and, if you're really lucky, stabbed with a pair of safety scissors. Face it, your ego would much rather be stroked than suffering public bitch slaps, but experiencing them will soften your heart to those around you and allow you to find true compassion. We don't all fight the same battles in life or business, but we all do fight battles, and we all owe each other compassion rather than judgment.

7. Failure helps us gain a better perspective around the almighty dollar

I can honestly say every time I have failed, in some way it has improved my perspective on money. You see, through failure what you value becomes much more clear, and with this comes a deeper awareness of how you want to spend your money. Once you align your values with how you spend money, things become more simple. You start to spend less because you cannot possibly value everything you currently spend money on.

For example, I moonlight as an interior designer and my home is (obviously) my favorite canvas. I have fallen victim over the years to just buying things for the sake of buying them, for the five-second consumerism high. Perceived failures in my business have led me to cut way back on experiencing these frivolous highs. But that, in turn, has allowed me the chance to re-evaluate my home and the things I bring into it. Slowing the roll on the "stuff" I have brought in has allowed me the chance to breathe and envision what I want my family surrounded by.

I have built a design bucket list and I'm slowing down in actualizing it. Allowing myself the option to see the bigger picture without drowning in all the random stuff allows me to make the best decisions. My design and my bank account reflect this re-evaluation. It's easy to get bogged down by details and miss the big picture. You wanted your home to feel like Palm Springs glam, but all of a sudden you wake up and your home is tropical, boho, farmhouse (thanks, Joanna Gaines), modern traditional and you don't know who the f* you are anymore. It's OK to want things; it is also OK to press pause and reflect so that you stay true to yourself and your wallet.

8. Failure shines the light on who our true friends are

I think we all have experienced some friend editing along the course of our lives. I have learned very quickly who my true friends are after I have experienced failure. But sometimes it's not even about failing when you see some friends fall by the wayside. Sometimes it's just when your life might begin to be a bit too messy for their liking. Unfortunately, failure becomes an effective "friend filter" at times.

Most people are programmed to go toward the path of least resistance and gravitate toward what's easy. If things are hard, a lot of people will take a pass. I know for me when my daughter, Marlie, was experiencing seizures and was at the height of some her medical issues and setbacks, we stopped hearing from some of her friends and their parents. No matter your age, we are all susceptible to being pushed aside when our reality isn't as fantastic as others would like. We are all trying to escape reality to some degree and friendship is not spared from the brutal fight for escapism. It is a hard truth, but it's reality. Our struggle was just too much for some people to cope with. But true friends love you for who you are no matter where you are in life or what you are experiencing—the good, the bad, the ugly, the seizures—they are there. That's a friend.

9. Failure helps train the mind

Failure gives you the chance to train your mind to focus on the opportunity of what lies ahead rather than the perceived loss incurred. The mind is very much like the lens of a camera—it will see whatever you focus on. If you focus on what was lost, then that's where your mind will be. When you train your mind to focus on the right things, you can better cope with the disappointment of failure. This is where acknowledging what you are thankful for and having gratitude helps. Focusing on what you do have rather than what you don't have is essential in getting your mind to work for you rather than against you. Start journaling what you are thankful for, start reading positive daily affirmations or listening to uplifting music—all of this and more will help your mind stay focused on what you have to gain rather than what's lost.

Also, another technique I've used to get me through hardship is practicing a form of therapy called CBT (cognitive behavioral therapy) over the past several years while dealing with some of my challenges. It's based on the idea of reprogramming our unhelpful thoughts and behavior patterns by creating positive coping strategies that target improving our cognitive functioning. Once a negative thought enters your mind and you find yourself going down the dark, destructive road of fear, CBT allows you to push pause and ask yourself some questions. One of the most often used is "What proof do I have that (fill in the blank) even happened or is actually that bad?"

This might sound silly, but sometimes creating a simple pause in our thought process prevents us from ending up in a full-on anxiety attack. I try it as often as I can, but I need to come clean and tell you that when my daughter is screaming in my face because her ponytail is too tight at 8 o'clock in the morning right before we walk out the door to head to school, I find myself asking the wrong questions, like "What proof do I have that I really don't want to leave her in the street as I drive away right now?" I hate when CBT falls flat like that. But I keep trying!

It all starts with the awareness that your thoughts are prohibiting you from living a productive, fulfilling life, so take a deep breath, reset and begin again. (And please don't abandon your daughter!)

10. Failure reaffirms your faith

I think I've been pretty open that I am a spiritual being. As I wrote in my introduction, much of my drive and inspiration in writing this book came from my own spiritual journey. I felt compelled to share my wounds and pain with you and this book has given me the opportunity to do that.

My personal belief is we are interconnected beings and there's a spiritual fiber that runs through us all. It's natural to reach for your faith to allow you to go to a place that transcends yourself and the limited ego we all have. It allows us to realize there's more going on here than meets the eye. There's a purpose to our existence. We are more than flesh and bones; we serve a very calculated purpose in the world around us. Life, all failures included, is discovering that purpose.

When I feel desperately lost, my faith allows me to embrace the questions and find strength and beauty in the mystery of it all. There is an element of surrender that takes place when you hit rock bottom. It transcends all rational thought, logical analysis and deductive reasoning. It takes us out of our head and into our spirit. For me, this element of surrender is my surest path to peace and understanding. I've learned over the years that all my hustling, doing and being isn't always the answer. Beloved spiritual priest and teacher Henri Nouwen said, "Think of yourself as a little seed planted in rich soil. All you have to do is stay there and trust that soil contains everything you need to grow. This growth takes place even when you do not feel it. Be quiet, acknowledge your powerlessness and have faith that one day you will know how much you have received."

11. Failure helps you define what success means to you

Like I've mentioned before, success is subjective, so we first need to define what it looks and feels like for us (not what society, our friends or even our family tell us it looks like). Once we do this, we can redefine success for ourselves and begin to turn our failures to work for us, not against us.

Success starts to mean less and less when our values aren't aligned with our goals. Have you noticed that as you found success, the smaller joys tend to disappear? Things that used to cream your corn just don't anymore? Getting to go on work trips all of a sudden feels like a chore instead of a huge experience. Being interviewed by the press feels like a time suck instead of an honor. Eating out every night feels basic, when we used to dream of days when we wouldn't feel guilty picking something that wasn't on the dollar menu. When things become commonplace, they lose their luster and we lose our sense of wonder and gratitude. Our aim should be to find success without losing the ability to find joy and validation in simple things.

12. Failure helps you focus on how to spend your time

Some say time is our greatest resource. No one has more or less time than anyone else. So, it's up to us on how we spend it. Again, this goes back to what we value. Just as I said with money, the same goes for time. How you spend your time allows you to take a hard look at what you value. Time management that's aligned with your values is crucial to learning how to get what you want and need. With that said, be kind to yourself. It's not always going to be perfect and you are going to go through certain times in your life where your time is focused more in one area than another. But that's OK because sometimes what's needed trumps trying to achieve a perfect balance.

For instance, when Marlie was deep in her struggles a couple of years ago, I pulled back from work in a pretty significant way. I was solely focused on figuring out how I could help my daughter. And my business suffered for it, but I don't regret it. My soul, my heart and my daughter needed me. When I was ready to join the troops in the office, I did. Finding my groove again was tough, but there was an awakening within me about my career and the role it plays in my life that I would not have realized without some very intense struggles.

13. Failure makes you more passionate about your mission

As I've been saying this whole time, if you failed, it's not the end of the road—**it's a new beginning**. A chance to pick yourself up and try again, but here's the good part: This time is different. This time you are armed with all the knowledge, wisdom and experience you garnered from the previous "failure." You now have an opportunity to become even more passionate about your mission, about the NEW way to your truth. It's a way of refining the ideas in your mind and solidifying them. You might even allow yourself the space to reinvent your mission, edit it—or even start over from scratch. It is a kind of cleansing, a cleansing that allows you grace and time to find what works and WHY you believe in it. And with so much passion, you can almost taste the success!

14. Failure brings you closer to community

It's hard to go through failure alone and for many of us our natural inclination is to recoil, fall into bed and give up. A sort of paralysis seeps in and it becomes easier to lie there instead of fight to get back up. We even tuck our tails and purposely ignore phone calls and texts—really any form of communication that reminds us what we failed at. But we MUST ignore the pull to isolate ourselves. I can say with 100 percent certainty that whatever you have failed at, someone else has, too (and between us, maybe they even failed worse than you did).

Our lives might be unique, but stories, like fashion trends, tend to repeat themselves over and over again. And those stories exist in other people's lives as well. It's important to share our stories and experiences. Our stories have the ability to not only heal us, but can heal others, too. There's a freedom that exists in telling your story. I dare you to tell your story and watch what happens in the room. A weight lifts and all of sudden others feel free to acknowledge and share their own stories. This is where community comes in. There is a collective spirit that surrounds us and wants to help. We just have to open our hearts and minds and answer the call.

Through my own failures, I look to strengthening my bond with people in my community. I reach out. In fact, this book is a form of reaching out. I'm telling you what I am going through and you know what? It feels good. As much as I worry about what people will think, it's still not worth shutting myself off. I mean, yes, there are always going to be haters (*And the haters gonna hate, hate, hate, hate, hate . . .*), but that can't stop us from coming together to help one another by sharing our stories and being REAL. Maybe there should be a Failures Anonymous so we can all rebound together. I'll bring the coffee and all the dirty, ugly failures—but only if you bring yours, too!

15. Failure helps you recognize your strengths and weaknesses

They say nothing changes unless you do. When you experience perceived failure, you learn to recognize your bad and good qualities and habits. And when success means enough to you, you begin to change. You slowly modify your behavior over time to help rid yourself of any bad habit that was holding you back from success. You are forced to go deeper and bring awareness to where you can modify your behavior and be better.

I've had to face some humbling facts about myself as I've built my company. There was a time when we were experiencing a higher turnover than normal within our team. At one point a couple of years ago, I conducted an exit interview with someone I was losing who was vital to our team, and she said, "I like what you are doing here and I think you are an inspiring leader, but you never really gave me the tools to succeed and I felt like no one took an active interest in training me." Well, it was hard to hear, but she was right.

As an entrepreneur, I am built to ACT. I'm built to be scrappy. I am built to problem-solve. I am built to get the job done. Entrepreneurs have a tendency to be very tunnel-visioned on how they see achieving their goals. And unfortunately, some people who work with us can find themselves sidelined into feeling too much autonomy. While many entrepreneurial traits are admirable and get you to a certain point of success, there does come a time when you have to stop and invest your time and energy into others. There comes a time when you need to build longer-term systems and processes where people feel supported and set up for success. I cannot deny that we are still working on improving this aspect of our business. Our reality is often too reactive than we wish. But this feedback brought to my awareness that we needed to work on this, even if it hurt hearing it.

16. Failure inspires us to never give up!

When I think of the idea of never giving up, I think about what Winston Churchill once said: "I believe in courage, and I think it's the virtue that ensures all the others." Never giving up requires us to get past the fear of failure and do it anyway. Yes, it's scary, but don't you always feel better about yourself when you've done something scary? I have discovered this part of myself in writing this book, giving public speeches, having difficult conversations, designing products each season, running my company and facing my worst fears with Marlie's challenges. Regardless of success or failure, I believe REAL courage grows out of the belief that something unbelievably worthwhile exists just on the other side of action.

I've also found that thrill and excitement and action go together. It's a lot like riding a roller coaster. The intensity mounts as you make the jerky, creaky trek up to the top of the hill. Your stomach is in knots, your heart is in your throat, but once you mount the top of the hill and find yourself on the other side, you get the most amazing rush. It's a high you can't duplicate without scaring the shit out yourself first.

Trust me, I often feel I have plenty to lose, but I do my best to show up every day knowing I have more to gain than I do to lose. Moral of the story is . . . no matter how many times you fail, keep pushing, keep getting up. No matter how many times your head tells you to turn back and seek "safety," listen to your gut and heart instead. Do something that scares you every single day and find yourself inching toward your ultimate goal.

Sometimes the Hard Thing and the Right Thing Are the Same

Writing this chapter has proven difficult. So difficult, in fact, that I had to have a little liquid courage to get it all out. As I mentioned throughout the chapter, I am in the middle of dealing with my own sense of failure. So even though I do believe what I wrote and do my best to practice what I preach, I need to be honest and tell you my story is still ongoing and the outcome has yet to be determined. I don't know exactly what will transpire with my company, but I do know that I am doing all I can to not only ensure it survives but also thrives, and doing all this without wrecking my self-confidence or sense of purpose. It has felt therapeutic for me to put all my vulnerable ideas and thoughts about failure down on paper, but it also brought up a lot of difficult emotions. (I guess I'm trying my hardest to put my knowledge of CBT and love of white wine to good use!)

But seriously, through all of this stress and crisis, I'm noticing something about myself. I tend to seek out listening to older music for comfort. Listening to an old song is like being with old, familiar friend who knows you so well that words aren't required. Music allows us to freely feel or remember another time when things might have felt a little easier and our dreams felt so right, so doable, so necessary. It takes us out of our heads and brings us back to our hearts.

Well, something happened the other day that felt like the stars were conspiring to help me. It wasn't by coincidence—or at least I don't think it was. I was in my car listening to music and an older song came on called "All at Once" by The Fray. I immediately recalled liking the song when it came out several years ago. As I listened, it slowly dawned on me that it was popular right around the same time I began opening stores. A smile came across my face as I sang along in nostalgia. But then something unexpected happened. My mind focused on a single repeating, central lyric, "**Sometimes the hardest thing and the right thing are the same**." This phrase seemed to elevate, even heighten, through my car's sound system. Well, this was it. That's what I felt, too, right there in that moment.

Those profound words found themselves piercing my heart. Once again music became like an old friend, comforting, supportive and telling me exactly what I needed to hear. I took it as a sign that I could move forward with courage and conviction, and even though what lies ahead might be hard, it doesn't mean it's not right. The song goes on to say, "Maybe you want it, maybe you need it, maybe it's all you're running from. Perfection will not come."

The sweetest victory is the one that's most difficult. The one that requires you to reach down deep inside, to fight with everything you've got, to be willing to leave everything out there on the battlefield—without knowing, until that do-or-die moment, if your heroic effort will be enough.

Well, Grandma, you were right. Life is a bitch, but I'd sooner die than give up on myself.

ASK YOURSELF

As much as we might want to move on from our latest perceived failure, it's important to evaluate where we might have gone wrong and what and how we can learn from the experience.

1. **What have been some of your more significant "failures"?** Write them down, along with: What led to them? What could you have done differently? How do you think you can change as a result of what you have learned? Did the mistakes you made lead you to question your values?
2. **Did your friends abandon you or help you through the crisis?** What about your family? Was it important to you to involve them, or were you afraid they might judge you as a failure, too?
3. **How do you spend your time and what do you spend money on?** Again, write down your day, and how you literally are spending each hour and minute. Are you indulging in a habit that takes

more time than work or family or things that bring you joy?

4. **Do you need to acquire some new skills or tools?** How can you do this? Remember, a perceived failure can be a powerful learning tool, but only if you take time to assess what led to it, and how you can change your behaviors, thoughts and actions to get closer to success next time.

The Big Four

The four big areas that trigger feelings of failure are divorce, money, losing a job and academic achievement. I hear so many people refer to these life events as "I failed," especially when it comes to divorce. Divorce is painful, and it's a hard one to keep to yourself. Everyone has an opinion. But really it does take two to form a relationship, work on it and then leave it when it's not working. It also comes down to the fact that you had the passion and the courage to create this partnership, and the awareness to let it go.

A perceived failure in the money department can lead you to an awareness that could change your life by clarifying what you truly value. Losing a job is devastating and can lead you to question your abilities, your choices, your competence, but often it gives you the opportunity to examine what you are doing, whether it's a good fit for you and to explore something different.

And academic achievement? Don't get me started. At the end of the day, most of academia is swamped by the idea that there is one way to teach children—that you educate high-level thinkers one way, and students who learn differently another specific way. One size fits all. Most schools don't prioritize visual learning in their curriculum. Therefore, many students fail to recognize and understand their own method of learning. Maybe it's because I'm poised at this moment: My son is going to college and my daughter is coping with her learning challenges.

The whole pass-or-fail structure can be disheartening, but I tell my children that our family's values aren't defined by these singular approaches, that we don't consider them part of our resume. So I'm hoping that the pass/fail harsh reality can be mitigated by parents who know we are so much more than that. Sometimes there is an unintentional laziness to buck the system instead of looking at what the real issues are. For instance, if my daughter needs 30 more minutes to sleep and does better that way, it's my job to see if that can happen, instead of just taking the easier way out. You have to be willing to resist.

* * *

Chapter 6

THE MYTH OF HAVING IT ALL

We share a delusion that there is such a thing as work/life balance. But it's not what you imagine.

I grew up thinking I could do it all. *Seriously.* I had strong matriarchal figures in my life. A strong mother and an even stronger grandmother. These women spent much of their time whispering in my ear to "Shoot for the moon!", "Go for the gold!", or my personal favorite, "You can be anything you set your mind to being!" And here's the odd part: I believed them.

I was the baby of the family. My exhausted mother thought I was an ulcer for four months until the doctor broke the news that her ulcer was me. She describes getting the news that she was having another child much like finding out you have a benign cyst on one of your ovaries—not overly concerned, but not looking forward to the removal of it. In other words, my mom was not expecting me. She already had two small children and an ambitious husband at home to contend with. Who knows, maybe I picked up on her dispirited energy while in the womb and it created a fire inside of me to make my presence known, appreciated and valued? So I came out roaring! (Mom, you can thank me later.)

But the reason I tell you all this is because these beliefs, credos, ideas—whatever you want to call them—were ingrained in me on a cellular level, I swear, *like in utero.* And if I'm honest, I think I was just plain built to believe I was Superwoman (my bad).

I truly believed I could be it and do it all . . . .

I truly believed I could create a life that involved being a mother, a career woman, a friend, a sister, a daughter . . . .

I truly believed I could create the life of my dreams while simultaneously retaining my slim figure and glowing complexion (sigh) . . . .

I took for granted that I was going to have a family, a beautiful marriage, an active social life and an incredible business. I know what you must be thinking: *Is she a dumbass or what?* If I'm being honest, I *was* a dumbass. A young, idealistic dumbass, to boot, who bought into the bullshit. Being a Generation X-er, it's hard not to comply with the idea that this *impossible paradigm* can work. We were the ones coming up from behind the female pioneers (Gloria Steinem, Sandra Day O'Connor and Betty Ford) who so valiantly set the stage for female equality. And as I mentioned earlier, I am a pleaser and I want to do good by the women before me who fought so hard to give us these choices. I've clung to the idea that I cannot drop the flag for the next generation. No way. Not me. Not in my house (or office).

But let's face it. It's a shared delusion.

For all of us there comes a time or moment when the "I am woman, hear me roar, I can do it and be it all, I can control my own destiny and create the life of my dreams" begins to shatter, or shall I say takes new shape. For some it might have been your first job after college when you realized the working world was cutthroat and unforgiving. For some it might have been the first year of marriage when you realized the compromises you needed to make were bigger than anticipated. For some it might have been on your 35th birthday when you recognized there was no man or C-suite in sight. And for some it might have been the third time you missed a parent/teacher conference because of work.

For me, it was giving birth to my first child, Harrison. It was beautiful and traumatic.

Giving Birth to a Big, Fat Baby Shattered My Dreams of "Having It All"

I think of myself as a relatively self-aware, evolved person, but having a baby is the gold standard in gaining an immediate, instantaneous and sometimes humbling new perspective. Just to give you a little backstory and set the stage for how and why childbirth knocked me off my "I'm going to kick ass and take names" high horse: Having a baby almost killed me and my baby. Yep. Seriously. It did. And when you think you and your baby are going to die, you tend to get real, real fast.

I was in labor for more than eight hours and was in immense pain throughout the entire process. My doctor later told me I was experiencing a very rare condition called a "hot spot," which is a code phrase for a part of your body that didn't take the epidural. In my case, it was my lower right pelvic region. It felt like hot pokers were securely stationed in my pelvis. I was having hallucinations of cowboys sitting around a campfire heating up their red-hot pokers as I lay there awaiting my fate. I was struggling to stay sane and conscious.

When my doctor finally arrived at the hospital, she came in and took one look at me and announced, "She's in too much pain, we need to get this baby out now." I immediately thought, *No shit, lady,* and I started to push. I pushed more. I pushed again, but to no avail. He was stuck. She very calmly started to panic and shoved her hands so far up inside of me (I swear I felt a tickle in my throat) and said, "Elaine, your baby's umbilical chord is wrapped around its . . ." and in that instant, all went dark. I thought, *Please God, do not say neck . . .* and then she said, "shoulders." A huge sigh of relief washed over me, but she went on to say, frantically, "He cannot get out, so I am going to try a forceps delivery, and if it doesn't work, we will be doing an emergency C-section." I said nothing. I couldn't. I was in too much pain.

All of a sudden I hear her shouting "PUSH! PUSH! PUSH!" Nothing still. His heart rate was dropping. I could see the intensity in my doctor's eyes. She was now pushing all sorts of ominous-looking buttons and people started to rush into the room. The hoards of people crowded around my crotch started to feel like an orgy I didn't want to be a part of. But even with the spotlight on my southern hemisphere, I couldn't take my eyes off of my doctor. She was in charge. She was my God in that moment. Everyone else was irrelevant. I knew instinctually my life and my baby's life rested in her hands. I saw her discreetly look at the only male nurse in the room and confidently nod. I remember thinking, *Was this their secret language to kill me and save the baby?* I felt like I was in the middle of a scene from *The Sopranos* and was coming to grips with my impending death.

She commanded him, "Get on top of her NOW and help me get this baby out."

The male nurse froze and said, "I don't think I can do that . . . what if Dr. So-and-So comes in and sees me? I could get fired."

My doctor sternly replied, "Get on her NOW!"

This entire interaction was surreal. My doctor ordering a young male nurse to mount me and physically push my baby out of my uterus was not how I thought giving birth for the first time would go. I had only pictured a couple of "heave hos" of my own, not a large male nurse heave-ho'ing on top of me. Honestly, I was so far gone at that point, I didn't care if they had decided to just crawl right up inside of me and yank him out. And just like that, the gentleman nurse proceeded to get on top of me and began pushing violently on my belly.

I started to scream.

I guess the 200-pound male nurse hoisted on top of me—along with two very large metal forceps—did the trick, because Harrison was born about three minutes later. He arrived a bit beaten up: blue, bruised and traumatized (me too, buddy). They instantly hooked his little body up on heart monitors, and all sorts of doctors and nurses began swarming and hovering over him to ensure he was going to be OK. At that moment, I realized, even in my drug-induced state, that I was no longer the focus, he was.

Later that night, Jim wheeled Harrison into our room in one of those plastic tray/car contraptions. I felt like he was being served to me for dinner. I was having anxiety. The combination of drugs, pain and trauma was sending me into a manic state of fear. Harrison was swaddled up so tightly, I was afraid he couldn't breathe. I kept asking Jim if he was 100 percent sure he was in fact OUR baby. Am I the only one who wonders how they know whose baby is whose? Let's face it, all babies look the same: None are very cute, unless red, pinched, alien-inspired features are your thing.

After I stopped battering Jim with a hundred questions, Harrison began crying uncontrollably. I could barely move; I had a catheter shoved into the giant hole downstairs that used to actually be separate holes, and an IV inserted into a vein in my arm. I felt helpless. Jim was trying anything and everything to calm our alien baby down. He tried heavy rocking, aggressive patting and fast walking. I can still remember him incessantly saying "Shhh . . . shhh" over and over again, and then, to my astonishment, Jim broke. He walked out of the room holding our baby and let out a helpless scream.

The nurses scurried in, and to be honest, they seemed a bit disgusted with our sub-par parenting skills. We felt betrayed. Didn't they know we didn't know how to do this? Why wasn't anyone realizing that just because we love each other, had sex and conceived a baby didn't mean we knew anything about what to do with it after it arrived? Wake up, people! After the nurses got Harrison to calm down, thankfully he started to fall asleep.

What happened next will remain imprinted in my mind and heart for the rest of my time here on earth. The room eventually fell quiet. Jim drifted off to sleep, too. I, on the other hand, could not even think of sleeping as the pain combined with anxiety and fear were too much. There would be no resting for Mama tonight and many nights ahead, for that matter.

Harrison was lying with his eyes softly closed, in his plastic bin like a hunk of meat in the deli. They don't feed you in labor; I was hungry, OK? To get my mind off feeling like I was a wounded lioness who might be ravenous enough to eat her own young, I began to focus all my attention on my new baby. I started to take a detailed survey of his facial features one by one. I began to realize the miracle of what had just occurred. I began to think of how dichotomous life's journey can be. How are we able to simultaneously experience all of life's blessings, goodness, glory and miracles knowing immense pain, suffering, needless acts of ill will, unanswered questions and confusion still exist?

I just had a big, healthy baby, and the day before I was organizing the nursery and finishing up last-minute work obligations. This day, I brought life into the world. In some ways I can see how childbirth is seen as an ordinary miracle. It happens several hundred thousand times a day. But for a new mother, it's extraordinary. When it's happening to you, you feel as if you are the only person on the earth capable of such a feat, such an honor, such a right of passage.

As I lay there pondering this irony, I started to take even a closer look at Harrison's mushed face and I asked him very quietly, "OK buddy, what do you have in store for us?" And I swear on my grandmother's grave, in that instant his eyes gently opened. He gave me the stare of a lifetime. A glare that penetrated my heart. He didn't blink. It was as if he were looking straight through me, and right there, I knew the answers. I felt a strength of spirit emanate off of his tiny body. I felt like he was trying to tell me something. It felt like this: "Hi Mom, I'm here. It's going to be a wild ride, but I will be with you the whole way." I felt understood, comforted and loved. I knew I was going to be all right. But I also knew I wasn't ever going to be the same. (And neither was my vagina.)

All those trumped-up dreams, wishes and expectations from my past would begin to take new shape. A new life was beginning, for not only me, but also for my little family. A life with a broader lens ridding me of my own self-centeredness. A life full of constant editing and redefining of who I thought I was and who I was going to become. A life that might not look like the one I had imagined for the past 29 years, but the one I was supposed to live from that day forward.

Having It All: Moving From "One Size Fits All" to "What Works for You"

So what does "having it all" even mean?

Let's start with where the term "having it all" originated. Research states it was coined in the '60s by Helen Gurley Brown, the late editor in chief of *Cosmopolitan* magazine. Her book *Having It All: Love, Success, Sex, Money, Even If You're Starting With Nothing* was a landmark bestseller in 1982. Brown edited *Cosmo* for 32 years and published several books, and guess what? Never had children. Her obituaries claim the couple was "childless by choice," but her husband David Brown actually had a son from a previous marriage who died in the '80s of AIDS. Helen Gurley Brown is widely acknowledged as one of the most successful women in publishing, ever. Did she have it all? I don't think she did. Nor do I think I do. For me, her book implies that women who stay at home and choose to raise their kids are living a life half full. If you ask me, that's insulting.

I'm not sure I want to have it all. Like having it all is some sort of mecca women are trying to reach. Let's redefine "having it all," or better yet, let each woman define for herself what the best version of her life might look like. I've learned over the years that it's not about a "one-size-fits-all" model (it never is); it's ultimately about a "what-works-for-you" model. What I mean when I say this is: Women need to take a hard look at their lives and their choices and begin to build a life that works for their individual situation. We can't put all women into a box and assume we all want the same things.

The problem with the phrase "having it all" is it infers that all woman have the same dream: to be a mother with a loving family and a successful career. In my eyes, "having it all" cannot be universally defined no matter how much society attempts to do so. The phrase needs to be redefined as "having the life of your choice," or as I said earlier, a "what-works-for-you" model. Having it all means different things to different people at different times. It's ever evolving, highly personal and not set in stone.

I do believe in some ways women can have it all, but it's not constant and it will never be perfect. But that's OK, because nobody has it perfect. As I wrote in chapter 4, being a mother doesn't suddenly require perfection. You don't give birth to a little human, then suddenly adapt superhuman capabilities of innate perfection. If anything, motherhood requires humanity, modeling for your kids that not everything is always picture-perfect, but that doesn't mean it's not awesome.

The idea of having it all has morphed over time for me. I cannot deny that when I was younger, I entirely bought into the idea in a literal sense. During my teen years, I was fortunate enough to have a role model who owned several fashion boutiques across the Houston area. Her name was Joann Burnett. She lived in the neighborhood where I grew up, and I was in awe over the life she had created. She truly seemed to have it all: the perfect husband, perfect kids and a perfect business. I always told my mom, "I am going to be just like her one day."

Well, that one day arrived after I gave birth for the first time, and it wasn't the life I had imagined. I had a wonderful husband (still do), a healthy baby and a promising new business, but something was telling me this life I so desperately wanted was not going to be easy, and quite frankly, it hasn't been. I have slowly come to understand my limitations, and how life has a tendency to be uncertain and unpredictable no matter what you do to mitigate unforeseen circumstances. You see, all those frantic attempts to control your own destiny start to gradually wane as you age. You become attuned to the fact that control is an illusion and it's useless to keep pretending. That's not to say you just lie down, let life steamroll you and say "f* it." It comes down to building the essential skills and attributes, instead of resentments, needed to get you through these hard truths.

Adaptability and grit are two big ones. When things don't go as planned, when you fall flat on your ass, or better yet, a 200-pound male nurse mounts you and metal clamps deliver your baby, the ability to pick yourself back up when you stumble or feel let down by reality is probably the single most essential life skill. The "having it all" myth doesn't seem to make room for these bumps (that we all wish a giant pair of Spanx could smooth out). The myth tells us to strive for the impossible and therefore set ourselves up for failure and disappointment, time and time again. Regardless of what we try to control, the harsh inescapable reality is that time is finite, so no matter how much coffee we drink or multitask-enabling gadgets we use, we are ultimately human and the sun sets and rises no matter what we do. We have to have the adaptability to manage the cloudy shitstorm days, and the grit to rise again with the sun the next day.

Going Viral in a Good Way: *The Atlantic* Article

I remember exactly where I was when I read the article by Anne-Marie Slaughter in *The Atlantic* called "Why Women Still Can't Have It All." I had bought the June issue at LaGuardia Airport right before I boarded a plane in 2012. I was heading back to Houston after visiting the showroom we had just opened in midtown Manhattan. At the time, I remember feeling especially vulnerable to Slaughter's words, as I was beginning to realize I was burning the candle at both ends. We were in hypergrowth mode at the company, signing expensive real estate deals, expanding our product offerings, hiring new employees. It was becoming unmanageable. It was also around that time that I was knee deep in dealing with my daughter's challenges and discovering her condition was not something she would simply "grow out of." I felt scared, exhausted and in over my head.

Once we landed, I immediately gave the article to my husband and told him to read it. That night as I fell asleep next to him, I watched him intently reading the article. Seeing him validate my need to feel understood meant so much to me.

Even though Anne-Marie Slaughter and I have vastly different career paths with vastly different experiences, mine being entrepreneurship and hers being high-powered government assignments and elite academic teaching posts, I was taken by her in-depth, thoughtful analysis of what is really going on with this idea of women "having it all."

And quite frankly, I related to her admission that early in her career she completely bought into the idea, because I did, too. I can honestly say I blindly walked into my career thinking it was possible, but what I learned is all the chanting, marching, mentoring and "leaning in" gets you only so far if society isn't actually set up for real change to occur. And she emphasizes our belief in what she calls "half truths" and how we tend to underestimate just how complicated the issue is. We tend to boil it down to women not being committed or ambitious enough, or how vital it is to have a supportive husband to help at home, or to do a better job of managing our time so the "having it all" eggs line up in perfect formation for achieving our goals. The imaginary, ever-elusive "having it all" credo creates a no-win situation, a futile goal, a catch-22.

And "Leaning In" Only Goes So Far . . .

Facebook's Sheryl Sandberg is probably the most famous woman to address the idea of having it all in the 2010s. Sandberg delivered what some considered a mind-blowing speech at Barnard's 2011 graduation, notably saying in part that when a woman starts thinking about having children, she doesn't raise her hand anymore . . . She starts leaning back. And while I think her book *Lean In* is meant to be encouraging, it didn't resonate with me as much as I had hoped it would. Sandberg's catchphrase seems to infer that women are the issue, that if we change our behavior to being more outspoken and not so confused, we would do better in the corporate world, when honestly it's sooo much more complicated than that. Her viewpoint seems limited. Where is the conversation around single mom's . . . middle class and disadvantaged women . . . minorities and alternate career paths like entrepreneurship? There are deeper forces at play around unchallenged societal norms and corporate America's attitude toward female roles. I'm just not convinced we are in as much control of our careers and families as we think we are. . . (there's that word again—control).

Please don't misunderstand me—I respect and admire Sheryl Sandberg and all she has done for women. Her courage to broach these hot-button issues inspires me every day, and I would go as far as to say even played a role in why I chose to write a book. My heart was broken when she suffered the most unimaginable tragedy, losing her husband so suddenly and unexpectedly back in 2015. I've seen her views soften and become more inclusive since that time, and I continue to be inspired by the work she's doing surrounding grief and trauma in her newest book, *Option B: Facing Adversity, Building Resilience and Finding Joy.* I guess what I struggled with the most in *Lean In* was how the book seemed primarily aimed at privileged, corporate, Type-A high achievers who have a goal of sitting at a boardroom table. Sandberg doesn't really step back to think outside of her own perspective to see how many women simply don't want to take this path or aren't in a position to. I've talked to many women who just want to be fulfilled, with good jobs they enjoy and that are sustainable both financially and emotionally, and who want to feel they can engage in the other roles they have in their life as mother, sister, friend, wife, etc. And while Sandberg does encourage women to make their partners *real* partners, she doesn't really ask the question of corporate America: How can businesses "lean in" to help women fulfill their full potential? Or better yet, how can we ALL "lean in" to help each other?

But again, kudos to her for taking on the myth of having it all. In *Lean In,* Sandberg writes: "Perhaps the greatest trap ever set for women was the coining of this phrase." Her premise is that increasing the number of women at the top of their fields will benefit everyone, and she asks men to be true partners, sharing in the family work that typically leads to a woman's decision to stay home; she asks women who expect to start a family soon not to check out of work mentally. And she acknowledges that there won't be straight paths, and writes that "It's a jungle gym, not a ladder" to explain the many different paths careers can take.

Leaning back doesn't mean you're giving up

I was with a close friend at dinner a couple of weeks ago. Of all my friends, she is the most career-driven. She is a ball buster. Strong, resilient, brilliant and quick-witted. She's the one I go to when my job feels hard. She gets it without judgment or fear of a heavy conversation. I was telling her about my recent challenges with the business and how hard a time I was having with closing the stores. I started to tear up and began to cry. She looked at me and said, "Elaine I know it's so hard when things don't go as planned but you have to trust there is reason. There is something awaiting you on the other side of this storm." She went on to say, "There are certain seasons for acceleration and certain seasons to pull in, reassess and reset." This is what I needed to hear as I was currently seeking shelter from a massive shit storm.

I began to tell her about my book and how much I enjoyed writing it. I told her about this chapter in particular and how freeing (and emotional) it was to write about the complexities of being a married woman with a career and children in today's world. I went on to tell her how passionate I am about honoring ALL women in ALL phases of their lives. My voice started to get louder and louder. I could see her eyes fixate on me. I am not sure if she was concerned we would get kicked out of the restaurant or if she was about to start screaming *"I am woman hear me roar!"* I ended my impassioned speech with: "Life isn't built on secure, predictable solid ground. Life is built on bumps, pot holes and quicksand at times. I want to start a movement for all women to join forces and *break their own DAMN glass slipper—whatever that barrier might be!* ***IF THE SLIPPER DOESN'T FIT THEN F* IT—GO BAREFOOT!"***

She looked at me with her eyes wide open—part stunned, part inspired, and to be honest I think a little afraid. It's not often people yell something other than "TEQUILA!!!" at a Mexican restaurant. But you know me, I carve my own path of women empowerment even over a plate of enchiladas. She looked down at her uneaten salad as if to ponder whether she should speak. She glanced up and softly said, "I've never really told you this before because I thought you would think I was really crazy or even worse really dumb. But I had a *Break the Glass Slipper* moment about a year ago. I had the opportunity to go back to work for a huge TV network and I turned it down, even though everyone around me was saying: "You are crazy, you need to jump on this, this is your Badass Girl Boss moment!" I just realized I have two adolescent children and a husband at the peak of his career. I just knew no matter how fat the paycheck was, I needed to stay right where I was. At this time in my life, I need freedom, sustainability and balance. Maybe I won't be winning an Emmy anytime soon but my heart and soul belong here with my family." We both hugged. We talked more about the proverbial glass ceiling and how even though the ceiling is in your reach, it doesn't mean it's time to break it. Sometimes it feels right to accept it, shit maybe even Windex it. And, if necessary *lean back* on it. You'll have your moment to break through it, when it's right for YOU.

Can I get an AMEN? . . . and a shot of TEQUILA?!

~~Work/Life Balance~~ to Work/Life Integration

It's the number one question people ask me: "How do you manage your work/life balance?" Well, I imagine, I am a lot like you. I take it day by day and make the best decisions I can based on what I know, what I value and what I prioritize.

Ironically, I am hunkered down in a hotel in Houston today finishing this book and it's my son Harrison's 18th birthday. So "mom guilt" is in high gear! I'm typing faster and faster to make sure I am home in time to watch him blow out the candles and eat a piece of cake with him. The good news is at this age they tend to want to do something low-key with family and the real party begins with friends. Or maybe I am just trying to convince myself I'm off the hook. (I'm a believer in developing coping mechanisms; occasionally rationalizing things away is a good go-to when desperate.)

I'm just going to say it: **I don't believe in work/life balance.**

The phrase implies that we must counter the downside with the upside. It suggests that we must tolerate and trudge through work in order to make a living, as long as we get to experience being fully alive, too. Why must we allocate half of our waking hours to something we dislike while nervously awaiting the other half to begin?

Furthermore, the simple fact that we call it "work/life balance" automatically implies that one of the two is negative and we need to balance it with the other—see, I already have a bad taste in my mouth. Why? Why are we pitting work against life? It makes it look like these two things are competing for your attention and well-being. In my view, work and life are not separate; they are the same. Work and life need to be integrated, not torn apart.

Let's start to say **work/life integration;** it sounds so much better.

I don't know about you, but a split, compartmentalized life is not a reality I want any part of. As I mentioned in earlier chapters, my work is a part of me. It's an essential component of my life's journey. It's about every step I took, every mistake I made, every success I had and every minute, every hour and every day I spent working so hard and so passionately to create something beautiful. My work has allowed me to create a life of meaning, contribution and purpose. Essentially, I believe all of that will be there with me as I leave this earth. It's a part of my soul. Confucius said, "Choose a job you love and you will never have to work a day in your life." My work has never been just about "what I do during the day to make a living"—it's been about contribution and offering my gifts to society.

However, I am in no way denying the fact that many of us are in dead-end jobs and show up for work strictly as a means to an end. Also, there are countless women and men who work two to three jobs at one time to just make ends meet. And if this is the case for you, this analysis could very well be superfluous.

Although for some, work might not be the entire problem. If you do feel your work is truly the main issue in your life and it's creating a sense of unease or imbalance, then I suggest you either reframe how you view your work situation or change it. I strongly believe that every person can make a living doing something they love. And often enough, it's more of a mindset to become happy with your work. It's often not the work that sucks, but how we see it.

I'm gonna get a little esoteric for a minute—please bear with me. David Whyte, a favorite poet and author of mine, talks a lot about the complexities around feeling integrated across all parts of oneself. In his book, *The Three Marriages: Reimagining Work, Self and Relationship*, he states, "The current understanding of work-life balance is too simplistic. People find it hard to balance work with family, family with self, because it might not be a question of balance." He goes on to analyze how we all share a very human, primal need to seek happiness. We all long for a feeling of wholeness. We all long for a feeling of being integrated across all parts of ourselves and our lives. I guess you could say we are collectively exhausted. We are told to have it all, balance it all and be it all, and we are losing our minds and hearts and happiness in the process.

If you ask me, *balance* is a tricky word. I would say work/life **IM**balance is the actual reality. The idea that we can balance it all also sets us up for failure, just as "having it all" does. A sense of imbalance is essential to our growth and progression as a species. I know for me, life isn't built on a scale. Life isn't fixed in a balanced state. I would argue there are seasons for imbalance in certain areas of our lives. For example, I've gone in and out of phases where I was hyperfocused on certain parts of my life, and then the vast horizon appeared and things began to open up to another view and my focus shifted. The issue rests more with being aware of yourself and the people around you than it does in achieving some elusive, idealized state of balance. If you are aware, intentional and mindful, you can and will successfully navigate the ebb and flow of life's disparate states.

I went through a phase at work not too long ago when I was way out of balance, overbooking myself and saying yes to every opportunity that came my way. Not only was I starting to become resentful about it, but I was depleted, exhausted and bitter, too. I couldn't keep up. It was affecting my psyche and my spirit. At first I was looking to blame the people booking me, but then I realized it wasn't about anyone else but me. I had to look inside of myself and realize I had some definite hangups about always saying yes and pleasing everyone. It's an issue, people! I learned that "No" is a full sentence and that I had to make the choice to create more healthy boundaries. So, this year I have been discerning about how I spend my time and what I choose to do. This way I can bring my best self to the people who need me the most.

The Beauty of Simplicity

This situation brought me clarity around the idea of simplification. I began to attempt to simplify my life and made a discovery. At first, I discovered myself channeling Marie Kondo, author of *The Life-Changing Magic of Tidying Up*, and going through each family member's closets asking myself "Does this bring me/them joy?" But after all the closets in my house were clean, and my family was thoroughly pissed off at my essentialism, I learned that simplification doesn't always involve stuff or work commitments. I learned that once I decided what my life was really about, I was able to define the few priorities that truly matter to me: my family, my friends, my health and my work.

We spend too much time balancing things we don't need in our lives, which turns our lives into a satirical circus act. This leads me to believe that it's not about balance at all; maybe it's about simplifying, making better choices and creating clearer boundaries. And it's just as important to assign what needs to go as it is what needs to stay. It's healthy to shed old ways of thinking or doing which no longer serve you. Letting go of unrealistic expectations can propel you forward.

Speaking of letting go of unrealistic expectations and old ways of doing things, my work has a tendency to bring forth a lot of the—"I'll never be good enough"—grumblings within me. As I sit here today, my business is transforming and changing, many of the old ways of doing things are falling by the wayside. Witnessing this happen is like being on an emotional seesaw. One day, I'm devastated. I'm grief-stricken. I'm desperately trying to hang on to what feels familiar—old behaviors, things, people and places. The next day, I'm relieved. I feel at ease. I feel a little lighter and start to see a glimpse of what my life could look like moving forward—simpler, maybe even smaller but definitely more whole.

You see, what I'm learning is all this building, producing, hustling, achieving, moving and stressing wasn't building the right things. Yes, literally speaking, 8 stores were built this way, a large and highly capable team of employees were built this way, a wide array of beautifully designed and well thought out products were built this way. Yet, my foundation was shaky at best. I might have appeared extremely productive, but I was cracking. And what have I really built at all, if I lose myself in the process?

Today is a new day. A new beginning. I am beginning to see the light shine through my cracks to show me a different way. It's a grand invitation to let go and be reborn. I'm not exactly sure how it will all play out or where the bricks will ultimately be laid, but I know I'm being called to begin again. I know one thing for sure: I am not here to build only for external gain. I'm here to build my soul, my family and my capacity to wholeheartedly love those around me. There's no denying I'm a work in progress on the "simplify" and "let go" game, yet I'm determined to continue to remind myself of who I really am. I'm not what anyone else says I am. Shit, I am not even what I might say I am. I'm not my company, I'm not the products I create, I'm not this book nor the words in it.

I am love. We all are. (Now, how's that for simplifying?)

The Choices We Make are the Life We Create

Life is about choices. And those choices have consequences. Jack Welch, former CEO of General Electric, said, "There is no such thing as work/life balance. There are work/life choices, and you make them and they have consequences." So with that said, I am a believer in the idea that YOU are the ultimate answer on whether you have work/life balance or not. It's not about the company you work for. It's not about your husband's or boyfriend's work schedule. It's about YOU, and doing the work to figure out what choices you are making and how those choices affect your entire life and possibly your future.

We are all different. We all have different lives and different needs and live in different situations. But where we are probably the most alike is in how we all desire supportive, fulfilling personal relationships. If the relationships in your life are a mess, it's probably safe to say other aspects of your life are at risk: career, health, finances, etc. Every single thing we do affects something else.

Sorry, folks, but life isn't a compartmentalized operation. It's messy, confusing and unpredictable. It's forceps and screaming on a day that was supposed to look like a Johnson & Johnson commercial.

Better Together: Millennials, Me and Meeting in the Middle

Have I mentioned how much I love generation talk? I geek out over talking about characteristics that define generations. It's like astrology; we lump people—based on birthdate—into a population that, broadly speaking, thinks, acts and interacts in a way that is directly related to the generation they were born into. It is f*ing fascinating.

Being in the fashion industry, I have had plenty of millennials walk through my door, take up residence in my studio, and teach me a thing or two about their views on work/life balance and Tinder. (Oh, but that's for another day.)

Work/life balance seems to roll off their tongues without much thought during interviews and developmental reviews. The younger generation is especially tuned into the idea. I've learned a lot from the women who work with me. They're young, pretty much part of Generation Z (aka millennials) and are generally very advanced in how they approach their lives. They have ideas about how to create a life that is fulfilling, and it doesn't always have to do with money. They seem to innately understand that the role models they were given with baby boomers and Generation X are not how they want to live.

I do wonder if they witnessed their parents, the baby boomers, trying to burn the candle at both ends, not succeeding and being very stressed about all of it. Or maybe the overstimulation of advancing technology has led them to always be searching for the bigger, better, best of everything.

They have taught me a lot about their sensitivity around the issue, and I often hear statements such as "I need to find a way that works for me . . . ." I am in awe over their ability to question and ponder such vital concepts at such a young age. I just remember saying yes to everything my boss told me and feeling like I had no voice or stake in any matters, much less my views on constructing a balanced lifestyle. I mean, the only balancing I did was my checkbook . . . ah, shit, let's be honest, my dad did that . . . so I, in fact, did no balancing of anything.

I do think people my age tend to get defensive about millennial thinking, and being a Generation Xer, I often don't relate to them, either, but when I take a step back and begin to see things from their point of view, I start to understand more clearly. I begin to see that I was not raised in the same time or circumstances they were. I didn't have the distractions of 24-hour news feeds, invasive social media posts and ever-changing, rapid advancements in technology that seem to change faster than the speed of light.

I came from Generation X, or I as like to call us, the "go play with the garden hose" generation, whom many refer to as "late bloomers" or even "late to launch." We are often stereotyped as having low self-esteem and lacking a clear-cut identity. It might be due to being sandwiched between two much larger, and some would argue more consequential, generations: millennials and baby boomers. But the one thing I do love about my underrated generation is *we were free.* Free to just be. Free to let our minds wander and experience emotions as they appeared. Free to engage in the full spectrum of human experience because, quite frankly, we didn't have our smart phones to distract us.

As much as I am a proponent of empathy and putting yourself in someone else's shoes, it takes two people to invest the time and energy into one another for real progress to be made. So, I also encourage my team members to attempt to understand *me* and where I come from. It can't be one-sided. It's essential, and at times it's very difficult for young people to step outside of themselves to see another way or perspective. I know it was for me when I was young.

I do my best to teach them that it doesn't have to be a work vs. life situation, and that they can look at their lives more wholistically. They tend to come at it a little differently than we older people do, like an "I'm afraid you're going to drag me down" type of mentality. I tell them life is not binary. It's not me vs. you. At its best, a working relationship can and should be a two-sided, mutually beneficial bond. Some older people see the millennials' views as unearned entitlement, but I think they see what we went through, what their parents went through and what they have experienced thus far, and are seeking real change.

I think we can all redefine exactly what it means to achieve work/life balance and come together with a healthier, more accurate idea of what it is we are all striving for. It needs to be a more customized approach so we can all can accept, adopt and tailor "what works for us" more effectively into our own lives.

My hope is that the younger generations learn to build the framework they so desire, and do the self-work to find the answers they seek that will improve their lives with regard to finances, self-reliance and emotional fulfillment. I see them seeking simplification, to be set free from the chains of a culture based on overstimulation, scarcity and "faster is most certainly better" ideology. They are reassessing the 21st-century maze we are all so desperately trying to escape.

And maybe they will learn some of the same things I have along the way . . . to simplify and edit out the things that are not bringing them fulfillment, to build resiliency when life knocks them down, to remain open and collaborative with others who support them and to have the self-awareness it takes to know when to change or adapt their situation.

The good news is I am encouraged as I witness society—and especially millennials—begin to debunk the idea of "having it all." The younger generation does seem particularly tuned into the idea that there needs to be an inherent flexibility in how each individual defines that. I believe as a society, we are progressing toward breaking down stereotypes and barriers, and working for the things in life that make us fulfilled and ultimately free to choose the life that best suits our own individual needs, wants and circumstances.

Now that, to me, is truly having it all.

Chaos, Compromise, Hope and Change

I think my experience with women over the past 25 years has led me to a more profound understanding of just how complex being a woman in the 21st century can be. I hear from many women in my life who feel as if they aren't giving any part of their life 100 percent. They feel they're "half-assing" it. I believe this notion of "half-assing" it contributes to much of the depression and general unhappiness we tend to see in women today, especially middle-aged women who are both working full time careers and are mothers—you know, the ones we've been talking about this whole time. And as far as I can tell, this is the only context in which a woman having half her ass leads to depression instead of daisy dukes. (Cue Jessica Simpson . . . .)

Seriously, though, all of the women I know recognize and value that we aren't relegated to the same narrow path as our mothers and grandmothers were: Get married, have babies, cook dinner and *voilà*!—success has arrived. It was those women, after all, who experienced more limited roles and fought so hard for us to have the myriad of choices we have today. But if I'm honest, ***I'm not sure***

we are happier. (I know . . . insert Pac-Man dying sound here. So depressing.)

In some ways it sounds whiny, even ungrateful, to complain about our plight. We feel guilty for complaining, but we don't know what else to do. What's hard is we had such high hopes for ourselves. We were the ones told we were going to "have it all," kick ass and take names. In my case, my mother and grandmother told me this, but it was also preached to us through our much admired female pioneers and the women's rights movement.

One thing does seem for certain: There are no perfect solutions to our complex dilemma. We have more choices, but we don't know what to choose. My therapist once told me that she could sense I was having a lot of uncertainty around specific areas in my life. I kinda looked at her and chuckled as if to say, *No shit, woman, what's your point?* And then she said, "Uncertainty is one of the leading causes of pervasive anxiety disorder. When you don't know exactly what to do, it creates a deep sense of unease and insecurity." I know this might sound obvious, but this awareness (and an antidepressant) actually helped me, because I realized that day as I walked out of her office: *I'm not crazy; I'm just not sure what the hell to do.*

Maybe it's OK for us all to admit that these choices don't make life easier. Possibilities create pressure.

Maybe it's OK to know we are in transition with how this women-and-their-roles and "having it all" thing will turn out.

Maybe we aren't supposed to figure it out yet, but that doesn't mean we aren't making progress.

And even after we analyze and reanalyze all the reasons, it's so dang complicated for women today: getting married later; having babies later, which makes you an older mom and inevitably takes you into serving multiple roles at the same time—i.e., raising your own children while putting your parents into assisted living—all while going through perimenopause.

And that's just on the home front. What about adapting to changing job markets, trends of freelance work and side hustles, the very real gender gap that still exists, unexpected financial recessions (or worse yet, unexpected personal financial crises), crazy presidents, keeping up with technology, all those damn millennials . . . and the Kardashians (shhh, guilty pleasure)?

We could spend hours discussing it all, but I am not here to do that. I'll leave that up to Anne-Marie Slaughter (she's so good). But I am here to offer a new way of looking at it. What it boils down to is how we choose to see it. I am not trying to simplify or dumb down this very real female epidemic of unease about our lives and our future, but I do think there are things we can do to manage better within the fear shitstorm.

Here are a few positive ways to reframe our plight:

We live longer and are healthier than the women before us, so we have a longer time to figure the life thing out. Aren't the 50s the new 30s? I'm choosing to buy into that, thank you very much.

Let go a bit. I do think we are one of the most intense, super amped-up group of women to ever walk the planet. Maybe we need to start to lighten up. Not take ourselves so seriously. As long as you and your loved ones are healthy and safe, isn't that the most important thing? You might be 10 pounds heavier, not have as much money in the bank as you hoped and have hot flashes on the regular, but so what? Remember: Life isn't lived to be controlled; it's lived to be lived.

Simplify your life! When possible, take an inventory of your life and see if there is room to edit or simplify. Do I need to volunteer on that committee? Do I really need a housekeeper three days a week? Does my child really have to take that extra piano class on Saturday?

Live in the moment. Acknowledge the beauty in the ordinary moments. Play Uno with your kids. Eat dinner with each other. Watch *Seinfeld* reruns together. Those are the moments where magic resides.

Celebrate the small wins, always. This is a big one for our family, and I know I've mentioned it earlier, but I felt it was worth saying again. Don't pass over your child getting into college. Celebrate! Don't pass over getting to school on time three days in a row—celebrate! Don't pass over not drinking wine one night a week—celebrate!

Progress, not perfection: Let go of mom guilt. We all seem to be wired for it, but there is a way through it. I'm feeling it now—remember it's my son's 18th birthday today and I'm sitting here typing in a hotel room. I know so many women who agonize about missing anything, especially those little developmental milestones: a first step, a first word, a piano recital. Whatever is fulfilling a mom emotionally, physically and intellectually is usually good for the kids. I believe in energy. If you come home emanating positive energy, your child will feel that. If you are making the right choices, responsible choices, then your vibe will tell your children that. I missed a lot of things I wished I hadn't, but when I looked at the day, I knew my decision was essential to what was needed that day. Maybe you miss a word or a step—you will see another . . . AND who knows if it was the first anyway?

I'll close with the topic of change. The one thing that's constant in life is change. And the one thing that is certain is "it all" is always changing. There are times when you might feel like you have everything managed and then there are times when you feel like things are falling apart. Your life circumstances will change. Your health will change. Your kids' needs will change.

So there will be times when you feel like you are plateauing or stepping aside and moving more laterally. But that's OK, too. As long as you've figured out a way to survive and meet your own needs and the needs of your family, you will be OK.

We shouldn't be so hard on ourselves for accepting that there is only so much we can do. You don't have to be perfect. You don't have to have it all. You don't need to do everything all at the same time. It's fine if you only have room for a few things in your life at certain times.

- **Be OK with plateaus.**
- **Embrace mistakes.**
- **Discover new paths to get there.**
- **There's never only ONE right way—there's only YOUR right way.**

ASK YOURSELF

Some myths will not be abandoned; they insist on staying with us. The "having it all" myth is one, and it's why I struggle with it. There might not be any solutions, but self-awareness, flexibility and the ability/desire to live with the messiness are good starters. Take a look at your life and what you want from it:

1. **Where are you in your career and family journey?** What do you imagine it will look like? How will you get there?
2. **Do you have a partner?** How do you foresee them helping? How will you broach the subject with them?
3. **Think about your childhood.** Did both of your parents work? Did you feel neglected in any way? Do you think these aspects of your childhood have an influence on the choices you make?

* * *

Conclusion

IF THE SLIPPER FITS . . .

As Queen Bey says, "Who Runs the World? Girls."

You know that feeling you have after a badass "girls' night out" where you drank too much, said too much, cursed too much and maybe even cried too much, yet, after you leave, a feeling of euphoria washes over you. That's how I feel right now. Writing this book has been cathartic; sharing all of these thoughts, ideas, beliefs, myths (whatever you want to call them) with you cracked me open, and when you get cracked open, the light seeps in. And when the light comes in, the darkness dissipates and you begin to feel more connected to your true self. I feel like I've been hooked up to the best kind of happiness hormone IV drip this past several months, and girl, I feel "drunk in love." I feel like now you and I have our own circle of trust. I've shared (maybe even overshared) my heart and soul and lessons I've learned over the past 45 years of trial and error.

I'm not perfect (unlike Beyoncé, I DID NOT wake up like this), and my journey has been far from perfect. But the awakening I had when I met the woman in Dallas battling cancer brought me a newfound awareness. An awareness that much of what society preaches as true is actually untrue. And with this newfound understanding, I have discovered a deeper connection to myself as I attempt to unravel the myths we are sold and told to believe as women. I guess you could say the beautiful woman in Dallas was like my very own fairy godmother sent to teach me things I thought I already knew. She didn't wave a magic wand or pimp my pumpkin ride, but she did ignite a spark in my soul. A flame I couldn't put out if I tried. A flame that I have used to get through some extremely vulnerable moments in my writing.

I want that for you, too. I want this book and my voice to be your fairy godmother. I want to release the power and insight you already have within. I want to give you the freedom to know that you don't have to be bound and helpless like Cinderella, and that fashion isn't frivolous (even Cindy needed a dress for the ball). And though it's hard, I want you to forget the evil stepsisters and free yourself from feeling like women are your rivals. I want you to live the moments in your life for YOU, not for a prince or a wicked stepmother, because that is the only way you can ever really "have it all." And on your journey to having it all (whatever "it all" means to you), give yourself grace. Allow yourself the chance to be vulnerable. If you fall down, if you break, if you have to admit you aren't perfect, life will move on and it will do so in a way that allows you to find your truest self. I mean, shit, Cinderella had to have a fleet of mice help her with her dress. Even on your worst day, you'll never have to turn to vermin.

Life isn't a fairy tale, but it can be pretty damn magical.

So here's to you . . .

To the girl bosses and the CEOs of the household. To helicopter moms, cool moms, single moms and dog moms. To the women who feel like they are burning the candle at both ends working split-shift jobs and showing up late for T-ball games. To the women who intentionally chose not to have children, who live and breathe by grabbing a seat at the boardroom table or C-suite, and women who are gypsies and fully live a life of creativity and wonder. To the women who eat their feelings and refer to wine as just another one of their girlfriends (remind me to call Kim Crawford later). To the women who keep everything together even when it seems like it's all falling apart. To the women who dream and the women who think they have forgotten how to dream.

You are brave, strong and resilient. You have the power to change the world and the lies it tells us. But to do that, you have to bend and flex, ebb and flow. You have to shatter the stiff, cold glass slipper. The slipper that doesn't allow you to move with grace when life deals you a blow. The slipper that restricts your movement and squeezes you into someone else's idea of perfection. The slipper that makes you feel fragile and easy to fracture.

So, go on . . . shatter the glass slipper. It doesn't serve you anymore.

Break the mold by taking back the truths about who you are and what you can achieve. Push aside the myths, lies and bullshit that have you feeling "less than." Once you do, the only thing you'll fear at midnight is whether or not you have clean underwear for tomorrow.

No, but really, maybe go ahead and stock up.

* * *

ACKNOWLEDGEMENTS

In Gratitude . . .

It takes a village to raise children . . . and write a book. Here's to the tribe who kept me going when I wanted to quit, inspired me, dove deep with me and never judged the f-bombs. (Well, my mom probably rolled her eyes a few times.)

Peg Moline, my writing coach, mentor and now newest friend. Thank you for being my touchstone while writing this book. You have guided me through the entire process and your unique combination of stability, calm, diplomacy, and unrestrained passion and zeal for this project has fueled my fire to keep going. I am particularly grateful for you talking me off the ledge at the very beginning when I was convinced I couldn't do it. Namaste, Peg. I have loved every minute of working with you.

Melissa Brandzel, for combing through the manuscript with a discerning and nonjudgmental eye (I hope my birthing story doesn't scare you off from meeting me in person) and doing the final copy edit.

Amy Cunha, my PR director/publicist, who pushed me to write a book in the first place! I can still remember us sitting in our conference room several months ago and you listening to me blab on and on about all of my thoughts and ideas. You stopped me mid-sentence and abruptly said, "Elaine you should write a book." Thanks, Amy—without you, this wouldn't exist (be careful what you wish for). And thank you to **Alicia Dunams** for deciding to take a chance on me and publish this book. I love your energy, enthusiasm and passion for women. Your energy is infectious. You are just an overall BADASS.

Mom, thanks for giving birth to me and encouraging my creative gifts. You are the writer in our family and I've been inspired by you since Day One. I'm grateful that you have supported me through this passion project. Your discerning eye with grammar and sentence structure has fortunately kept my book from being one big, long, run-on sentence. And thank you for helping me edit out superfluous cuss words when needed. I know seeing f* and shit has been tough on you.

Dad, thank you for always telling me that I'm the greatest human being on the face of the earth and that Oprah is for sure going to be calling me after this book comes out. There is nothing like having a father's unconditional love—even if it's a little biased. OK, a lot biased.

Trainor and Valerie, my brother and sister, who had the pleasure (and displeasure at times) of growing up with me. Thank you for being role models, especially with this whole writing gig. You guys are the ones I will always look up to when it comes to getting thoughts down on paper. I'll never measure up to your writing skillz . . . OK, that was annoying: SKILLS. I guess I'll never grow out of being your annoying little sister.

Caitlin, thank you for making my stories even funnier by not allowing me to forget all the crazy shit I've shared with you. Also, thank you for not walking away when I told you sad stories. You might as well carry a flashlight because you push me to explore the dark, to be better and more courageous with my storytelling. I am forever grateful for the influence you have had on me as a friend and a creative colleague.

Harrison, my wiser-than-his-years son, you have been so wonderful to support me with this project. It means a lot to me that you have read it and taken an active interest. I know a book about women is probably not at the top of your list (sorry in advance that I didn't write a book about the Astros winning the World Series). Being a damn good writer yourself, I welcome your advice. I hope you invite me to help you edit your own book one day.

Marlie, my bright light of a daughter, thank you for being YOU. You are the reason I wrote this book. Your light inspires all I do. Your existence has shaped my heart in ways I never expected.

My team at Elaine Turner: **Judy, Diane, Paul, Tamika, Jessica, Kristen, Amy, Evelin, Natalie, Johnna, Cynthia, Claire, Kasia, Tina and Myke**. I am grateful that you indulged my need to wear yoga pants to work for the past six months while I wrote the book. You even looked the other way while I had a second drink on Thirsty Thursday. I feel extremely lucky to have your support and encouragement with this whole book gig because I know it took me away from the office. You guys are the ones on the front lines fighting the good fight each and every day. We feel blessed to have you on our team.

Alyce, Jenna, Rebecca, Alison, Lisa, Beth and Jenny, my friends—nay, my soul sisters—for your constant support, telling me I could even when it felt like I couldn't. All the late-night talks, last-minute wine interventions, Saturday spa days got me through this. I love you all more than you know.

Last, but not least, thank you to my one true love . . .

Jim, my husband, confidant, support hose—I mean, system—and my greatest treasure. Thank you for bringing me coffee, wine and carbs every time I was huddled up in my office trying to work on the book. Thank you for encouraging me to tell raw stories and to escape to a hotel every time I was on a deadline. Thank you for pushing me to my truest, most authentic self. You encouraged me to not shy away from what's true, even when it felt hard or involved stories about my vagina. Jim, you are my rock, my love and my heart. I LOVE YOU.

* * *

Made in the USA
Middletown, DE
08 April 2021